A SKY
OF MY OWN

MOLLY BERNHEIM

MACMILLAN PUBLISHING CO., INC.

New York

Macmillan Publishing Co., Inc.
866 Third Avenue, New York, N.Y. 10022
Collier-Macmillan Canada Ltd., Toronto, Ontario

Library of Congress Catalog Card Number: 59–9753

First Macmillan Edition 1974

Printed in the United States of America

PREFACE

T*oday*, more than ten years after I wrote this book, I sit on a stool in my laboratory and every few minutes I note the progress of my experiment, recorded in the window of my little black box. Over my desk, turning gently with the currents of the air-conditioned building, swings a model of Willie the Aeronca, made and given to me by my first student. Willie is gone, sold to someone, somewhere, and I no longer instruct. But the sky is still my own, and the Stinson carries me as of old, and it is as sturdy and elegant as ever, the envy of many pilots who now fly from the Hill. It is twenty-six years old, officially an antique, but it has a new engine, and pale cream paint and red trim replaces the deep red of its early years. It is the oldest of the planes in the hangar, although the casual observer would not know it; changes in aircraft design have been small over the quarter century. Planes are now made of metal instead of fabric, and most of them have a wheel on the nose for landing, instead of on the tail. This means better control on the landing run, but loss of speed in the air because of the increased resistance —the delightfully designated "parasite drag." Those of us who were born and bred on tailwheels are inclined to think that landing a nose-wheeler is a little too easy— compared perhaps to the automatic gear shift and the old stick-shift days—and the nose-wheel fellows, at least some of them, are privately loath to land a "tail dragger."

The big airport at the Hill is now quite crowded. However, the huge grass expanse, where prairie birds made their nests and quail ran at the edges of the ill-defined runways, has been attenuated, bit by bit. Now we have a paved runway, a long thin hard strip, and the other runways are closed. In the old days, in early spring, we would get bogged down in a sort of tundra, or we would land, splosh, in a puddle, throwing fountains of mud into the wings. So often we didn't fly. Now we can fly even after a downpour, but somehow, I regret the changes . . .

Elaborate and expensive radio equipment is now commonplace. Almost no one navigates without depending on the omnirange, the marvelous device which tells you exactly which compass course to fly, if you want to get there. Our first such device helped us to navigate over the Rockies. Our second, a really sophisticated beauty, is turned on before takeoff and off after we land. I could still navigate without it, but I wouldn't like to!

It is among the people of the Hill that the greatest changes have taken place. Poppa's heart went bad and he lost his license. He spent an evening in San Francisco with Bill, his favorite student now a TWA pilot, and made his last flight two days later, in a coffin aboard a jet piloted by Bill. Only a few of us remember him now.

He would not have enjoyed the changes for he loved to fly with the simplest of equipment, navigating by a road or river, or the iron compass (the railroad) and a watch, and he had no use for elaborate radios. And he loved the soft grass runways, where the grass blades tickled the wheels as he landed. One day, when a group of us had been teasing Poppa, and all of us laughing together, we stood in front of the hangar to watch him take off. He came straight toward us, on one wheel, at full speed. We scattered! He turned at the last moment and was gone, a demonstration of exquisite control. Now Poppa is dead, and we use only the narrow concrete strip, and the tires cry out their distress as they touch the hard surface.

Sturdy little Johnnie has grown up and gone, too. John now flies for EAL, tall and as sturdy as ever, and I was glad, on one wet and windy night, to know that he was at the controls of my flight out of Washington. I have not seen Albert in many years.

The Civil Aviation Authority of my early flying days has become the Federal Aviation Administration or FAA. Their annual budget is astronomical and some pilots of small aircraft feel that they play favorites. The lowly Cub is no longer welcome in the skies and is gradually being taxed and regulated out. There are now taxes on the use of the "navigable airspace" (does it wear out and need repairs?), taxes on gasoline, licensing and other things, and regulations for the mandatory installation of expensive radio equipment. All these requirements, which increase each year, make it hard for the little fellow who loves to fly but can barely afford it. And the

FAA never misses an opportunity to impress the legend of the crowded skies upon the uninformed public. Yet one can still fly over hills and fields across the country, from Cherokee to Currituck, and not see another plane in the air, except perhaps close around an airport.

Annual physical examinations for aircraft (Airworthiness Certification) and biennial ones for pilots have been FAA policy for years and rightly so. Years ago, however, a pilot's physical could be conducted by the family physician, who was likely to have some knowledge of the pilot's history, although little of flying. Today the physical must be conducted by a specially appointed FAA examiner, who undoubtedly knows more about flying but may hand out a medical certificate to a stranger. A large proportion of accidents are so-called pilot error. I wonder if these could be reduced by careful screening. There are accident-prone pilots around every airport. We all know who they are.

Part-time instructors are now scarce, for very few people, on a part-time basis, can teach enough students to satisfy the FAA or to face the elaborate flight test now needed for renewal of the instructor's certificate every two years. So the people who like to fly for an hour after work, and enjoy teaching and helping a student with his problems, and train perhaps a couple of students annually, are hard to find. They have been forced out by FAA regulations and replaced by the big, highly organized flight school.

With all teaching, but especially in flying, the teacher-student relationship should be a very personal one. And students learning to fly have special problems, and handle them in different ways. Teaching techniques which are useful in one case may be useless in another. The fear of being dropped is fundamental in all of us; for years we walk on solid earth (or concrete) and then we find ourselves supported, in empty air, by a structure as fragile as a paper sack. Of course we have problems. But now instructing has lost its individuality, and students are turned out in a pattern, by full-time, sometimes bored and indifferent, instructors. Perhaps a student will have several instructors during a few hours' flying time. Do these instructors ever tell a student, as I have done (tactfully, I hope) "You will never be a safe pilot?" I do not know.

For instance, there was Bob, professor of mathematics, who handled the Aeronca with authority and even elegance. Several times, just as I was ready to solo him, he would, as he would say later, "pull a boo-boo!" Maybe he would fly around the airport making right instead of left turns, or he would open the throttle when he meant to close it, and one day he actually tried to land downwind, into the path of an oncoming plane! I never soloed him. Another student had three minor car accidents on his way to the airport, and another, who seemed like a normal and reasonable person, flew like a raving madman when he was solo. Once I taught a professor of psychiatry, a tense and tight-shouldered person who hated to make a mistake. When his landings at the Hill were good, we went cross-country to Appleville, which has an enormous grass field, not flat, but rolling. He failed to handle the ups and downs, and managed several jackrabbit landings. I told him, we all do that sometimes. A few weeks later, at a hangar flying session, someone mentioned Appleville. "Where's that?" said the psychiatrist, and denied with undue vigor that he had ever been there!

My last student was also the best. He never made the same mistake twice, and he accomplished a minor miracle, making 100 percent on his first attempt at the FAA written exams. Late one calm evening, after we had flown several times around the airport, I got out and as I walked away, he turned and taxied the Aeronca to the end of the runway for his first solo. Then I saw a young woman running toward me across the grass. She flung herself into my arms, weeping and laughing at the same time. "Will he ever land? This is what he has longed for, all his life! Is he safe? Can he do it?" So the flight instructor comforted the student's wife and wiped her tears with a handkerchief while he flew, and even before I had time for my usual anxieties and doubts he was down and safe, taxiing happily toward us.

A few days later, I took the Aeronca solo, and flew every maneuver I had ever flown. Climbing turns and steep turns and slow flight, lazy eights and chandelles for elegance, spins and loops for pure fun. I thought of the day, so long ago, when the Agent gave me my instructor's rating, and Little Willie and I had flown so easily together. I landed as the sun, a fiery ball, disappeared below the horizon, and took off at once to find it again. One flight with two sunsets. On the way home, I stopped the car and sat for a while at the roadside among some yellow daisies, and re-flew each detail of my flight. And it was then that I knew with certainty what must be done. Home, I went straight to the telephone. "Come and get Willie the Aeronca. Sell it. Don't let anyone at the Hill buy it. Don't let me ever see it again." The decision was made . . . the end of an era.

In the central area of North Carolina which is our home, we are about equidistant from the sea and the mountains. I like to fly to the sea shore, to Cape Hatteras and the Outer Banks, where one can look down and see the shipwrecks on the shoals beneath the water, or to Kitty Hawk and the Monument and the rolling dunes, to remind me of the Wright brothers and the little boy who ran around shouting "They do'ed it! They do'ed it! Danged if they ain't flew!" And I never tire of looking at and wondering about those strange oblong depressions, dozens of them, scars on the coastal plain. The Carolina Bays. Some are now lakes and some are dry, many sizes but all the same shape and all oriented with the same northeast-southwest axis. No one knows what forces caused them, and from the highway one might never see them. From the air, one can only marvel.

Sometimes, on a fine Sunday, our compass heading is decided by the flip of a coin, and maybe the mountains have it. One day we flew to Roanoke, Virginia, to buy an ice cream cone! On one rare crystal clear day, we flew up the long range of the Alleghenies, over Maryland, and then we followed the Susquehanna for many miles. Destination, Ithaca. The mountains have ridges as sharp as razor blades, and the country below us was very wild, beyond the Williamsburg omni, a white tower set on a high hill. No landing places there, so our good Stinson must carry us over, until we reach the fields and houses of the Finger Lake country. A few days later, on our return flight, we started early, and at three thousand feet we were above the thick haze. The river was almost invisible and the sun was hot over us. As the haze level rose in the increasing heat, we climbed too, up and up to nine thousand feet. So we flew in the bright air, hour after hour, navigating by the omni, checking the time as we passed one omni and tuned in to another. Frederick, Maryland, Gordonsville and so on, till we picked up the familiar morse shout of RDU, Raleigh-Durham, and home. Below us, all the way, small cloud banks were scattered on the haze deck, and below and between them we could see the vague forms of rivers and roads in the dirty, stagnant air. We were alone in our special sky, clean and free and cool, and once, far away, we saw a tiny airliner passing by. With deep regret, when the shout of RDU was loud in our ears, we pushed the Stinson's nose down into the other world, and we were in the thick heat. Our special world was gone. Soon we'll find it again.

Durham, North Carolina
June 1973

To Aunt Dot

CHAPTER 1

In the beginning, I remember, it was just one sentence: "After the war, I am going to learn to fly."

The second world war was still in progress and we were teaching double classes of medical students. Life was not easy. It was complicated by the presence in our home of two refugee children as well as our own family. There were chickens in the back yard, a Victory garden, and food and gasoline rationing. These things gave me plenty to think about, so that when Frederick said it,

I took little notice. The idea, I thought, would be quickly and completely forgotten. It seemed too remote even to contemplate, too unreal to bother with. And yet . . . I should have known better. Frederick is not a person who makes idle, unconsidered suggestions.

"After the war," he said, "I am going to learn to fly."

Long ago, as a girl of seventeen or so, I had ridden for a few minutes in a barnstorming biplane whose pilot had set up headquarters in a meadow near my home. I remember the flight only as an ordeal. I was sick and giddy when the hills and the sky got all mixed up and out of place. I had no fun whatever. In the years since, I had thought of airplanes only as a means of transportation as impersonal as trains, or as much-hated weapons. Otherwise, they meant nothing to me. Flying a small airplane for fun was not an idea that belonged in my world, and, indeed, it was most unwelcome there.

Less than a year after the war was over, Frederick unexpectedly went off to an airport, to see about lessons.

"Darling," he said when he came back, "it's very easy. Lots of people are doing it."

He had seen the airplanes, flying round and round the field, practicing landings, and as he watched, a girl had arrived for her lesson.

"Quite a pretty girl, and in an ordinary summer dress," he told me.

He had arranged at the office for lessons, and was to take his first the next day. That day fear came into my heart, and up into my throat. I swallowed it down, and went off in a hurry to find something to do. But it kept coming back, high and tight in my windpipe. That afternoon I went off for a long walk by myself, to a hill with a glen under the trees where one can see out for miles across the valley, and there I scrambled to the top of a high rock, and sat and considered the mess. I had never faced a problem like this before. Never, in our eighteen years of marriage, had Frederick thought up such a wild scheme, nor had his approach ever been so definite. Never before had he given me so little chance for discussion of a project. It was such an incredible proposition, yet he insisted on treating it as if it were an everyday affair. I could only suppose that he knew how I would feel. He could never imagine that I would find airplanes congenial. I was much too conservative; too sure, all my life, that a new food would taste sour in my mouth. I was ready to try and do better, to give the unknown at least a chance . . . but not with airplanes. I swallowed hard, and started again my consideration of what to do. Was I going to try and stop it? Could I stop it if I decided to try? I was not at all sure, for I detected a strange, more-than-ordinary drive behind his gentle and reassuring words. And *would* I if I could? How can one love, and then erect a fence around one's man? I thought for a long time, as I sat there on the hill, and at sunset I climbed down from the rock and went home. I had made my choice, and I felt better, but the fear remained.

As it turned out, I had to live with it for a long time. It tightened in my throat at unexpected moments. I hated the days when lessons were planned, and rejoiced secretly if the chance of flying faded with the spreading rain. The minutes dragged toward dusk when I waited at home and Frederick flew. I dreaded the telephone bell, and listened hopefully for the sound of the car as it drove into the garage, followed by the welcoming bark of the old spaniel dog. And the fear came again, the next time. All that year, by mutual consent, and lack of understanding on my part, we hardly spoke of airplanes.

One day, after a long session of stall practice, Frederick came home and leaned against the door, grey with airsickness. And one day he ran in and hugged me, and his eyes were bright.

"I soloed!" he told me.

Still I didn't understand. How could I? The worst time was the afternoon when he came home later than usual. When he arrived, he was very quiet, and after dinner he was called to the telephone. I heard scraps of the conversation:

"The wing and landing gear? . . . Yes, of course I'll pay whatever it costs. . . . Yes, I know."

He had run the little plane off the runway, he told me later, trying to land it in a high and gusty wind. The gear and the wing had been bent. He wasn't hurt, not even scratched, and there was nothing to worry about. The damage could be easily repaired.

"One can smash up an airplane much worse than that, and not get hurt," he said, but I was not convinced. After that, I was more afraid.

I don't remember, really, how that year passed. A

sort of nightmare. I never suggested that he take me to the airport, and I never asked anything about flying. I was completely and utterly ignorant. A year and a day after his first lesson, Frederick went to fly and was gone for some time. When he came home, he was no longer a student pilot. He had passed his flight test and was now a "Private" pilot, and had the right to fly and take passengers with him, for the rest of his life. That night, sitting happily and quietly in his armchair, he spoke another unforgettable sentence.

"I bought an airplane today," he said. "It will be delivered in about a month."

There was a very long silence. Eventually, I spoke.

"Whatever," I gasped, "did you do that for?"

"Well," he said, "they've been very nice to me out there, and I thought I'd like to help them. And we'll have fun, too!"

And so, a few weeks later, the plane arrived. Frederick flew it with an instructor beside him. At first he found it difficult to handle, although he did not tell me so. Several times he came home quite discouraged because it was so different from the Cub in which he had learned, and he wanted so much to solo it. He explained to me that the Aeronca Chief had a wheel to control the elevator and ailerons, instead of a stick, but all that meant nothing to me, and I was not impressed. Presently he soloed, but all the time he said very little about it, while I thought a great deal. To me the thing was an unpredictable menace, a weight on my shoulders, a burden that I could not shake off. How I hated it! Of all the days of the week, it was on Saturdays that I hated it most. In the pre-airplane days, Saturday had been a day when Frederick and I had walked in the woods, or worked around the house and garden together: a special, pleasant afternoon when we could do the things we enjoyed, out in the sun and fresh air. Nowadays it was different, I thought sadly. Now, we would finish our work soon after lunch, and lock up our rooms in the medical school. The scientific journals would be left lying on the desks, and the used test tubes and flasks, containing the remnants of the last experiment, would be piled on the drainboard of the sink for the lab attendant to wash on Monday morning. Frederick would go and fly, and I would go home to wait for him. I would find things to occupy me, anything to keep me busy. The time passed better, I found, if I kept out of earshot of the hateful telephone bell. One beautiful October day, blue and white and clear as crystal, I decided that I would take the dog, and go for a long walk. My friends don't walk if they can help it, at least not what I call walking. They like to stroll and wander slowly along the woodland paths or through the fields. To them, two or three miles is a memorable undertaking. When I walk, I go fast and hard for eight or ten miles. It clears the restlessness out of my limbs and some of the turmoil out of my brain. When I come home and find the garage still empty, I can wait, as wait I must, with more equanimity. Frederick would still be in the sky, among those fluffy white clouds. What, I wondered, did he do up there? Did he have to work hard, to keep the airplane from falling?

With my jacket on and my handbag under my arm, I stood for a moment looking out of my office window, past the great magnolia tree that has leaves of polished green leather lined with brown fur. I could see the flagpole at the far end of the campus with the stars and stripes flapping idly, and groups of students moving in and out of the buildings. The sun was still warm, and the three tulip trees, turned to uniform honey yellow by the chilly nights, contrasted sharply with the dark pine woods behind them. Another Saturday had come, and another lonely afternoon was awaiting me.

As I stood there, looking out and considering these things, Frederick came and stood quietly behind me. He slipped his arm around my waist. Caught unready, self-pity welled up in me, and tears came into my eyes, to be blinked back and hidden. But it was too late. He saw them and understood, and I knew that he did. The moment had come.

"You'll be lonely, waiting for me at home," he said, "and I'll be lonely up there by myself. Won't you come and fly with me?"

He drove me through unknown parts of the town, far out into the country. We talked as we went, but not about flying. Once or twice I glanced at him, half expecting him to sprout helmet and goggles, but he looked just as he always did. Was it, to him, an ordinary Saturday afternoon, to be spent in the sky flying his own airplane? As we drove around a corner we saw a hawk swoop, with magnificent accuracy, and rise with a struggling rabbit from the roadside weeds. I did not wonder what it would be like to fly. How strange it was that I didn't!

At last we turned off the road and into a graveled parking area, and I saw a bank with a row of steps leading up it. On top of the bank were many people with their backs toward us. As we left the car, I heard a roaring noise that seemed to come from everywhere at once. It grew rapidly louder until an airplane came, skimming over the people, its underside exposed to our view. Heads swiveled around as the eyes followed it up into the sky. Over the road it flew, over the wires; the noise decreased and it disappeared. We climbed up the steps and through a gate in the white painted fence as the spectators moved aside for us. Children were sitting on the fence. I felt a stir among the people as we went inside, into the area reserved for the privileged. Then I stopped suddenly, for I saw coming fast and almost directly toward me, another airplane, on the ground in the track of the first one. Faster and faster it came and it raised its tail as it ran. Then the wheels left the ground and the roar of the engine changed as the plane swerved slightly and rose over me. And then I saw another, in the sky, sinking slowly down far across the field, getting bigger as it came. Silently it dropped toward us, without fuss or hurry, with enormous wings, two oblong eyes, and a smiling mouth, fringed with whiskers. It sank, with no break in the descent, peering, it seemed, at the ground ahead of it, until I thought it must crash into the earth; then at the last moment it raised its face to the sky, squatted neatly on the runway, and ran forward a short distance before it stopped.

I turned quickly to watch still another airplane behind me. It had been pulled out of the big shed, and I heard the engine, and saw the plane move away, yellow-colored with a red belly. It buzzed as it turned, and lurched clumsily. I thought: These things are not like birds. They are much more like fantastic overgrown beetles, awkward and ungainly, with hard shells, and they buzz like beetles, too. They seemed to waddle, with such great wide wings fixed stiffly onto them; like the one behind us, whose wing tips moved up and down in great arcs as the wheels negotiated the rough tufts of grass. Another one came from the sky, slowly down onto the earth. I thought it was the same one that had taken off as we arrived. The buzzing one, turning this way and that, moved out and away from the crowd. Presently, far in the distance, it roared extra loud as if in warning, turned, and charged us. What a mad, tail-high rush! It ran as a swimmer might rush to plunge headlong into deep water, sure of support. It ran with assurance of its own power, the power of flight, and plunged up into the air.

I stood, fascinated. I wanted to laugh and cry at the same time. Frederick was at my side, and with him a young man with brown eyes and a weather wrinkled face. It was his instructor, George. We talked for a few minutes, but I have no recollection of what we said. I sensed the eagerness of the crowd as it stirred behind the fence. A man and a boy stepped through the gate, and the man spoke to George about a ride. How much would it cost, to fly over the town?

"Can *you* make them fly?" the boy asked me. I told him No, definitely No, but as I spoke the words I began to be glad that I had come. I began to anticipate the headlong race, out over the wires, and the gentle and graceful descent to earth that would follow it. Would I laugh or would I cry?

Frederick and the mechanic were disentangling his plane from among the several that were still in the shed. It was pushed out, gassed and carefully checked. It was very small, yellow with green trim, short-tailed, and it looked too fragile to support two people in the empty air. I walked around it and touched it. The wings were high and thin, and cloth covered the whole machine, fine stuff that you could stick a finger through. And under the cloth? There was nothing, I was told, except a few wooden spars to keep the cloth from folding up!

We climbed in, sat side by side, fastened our seatbelts, then taxied out across the field to the long gravel strip that was the runway. Lurching, we moved slowly to the extreme far end, where we stopped. Then we roared loudly and turned. Far away I could see the shed, and the white rails and the crowd. We moved slowly toward them, bumping over the stones, increasing speed until the pebbles merged into one another, and the ride became steady and smooth. I saw our shadow, torn loose and floating, and the heads of the crowd, turning to watch us. And I saw the wires pass below, and our shadow racing ahead of us, over some cattle and over the hedge beyond them. The cars on the highway were like toys. The whole great countryside, huge and mottled with cloud shadows, spread around us. The earth was green, the sky was blue —in matching patterns—and purple blotches fitted closely under the fat, white clouds. Below us was a forest, lighted by pointed yellow candles in groups or singly among the pines; tulip trees, they must be. We climbed on, up and up. As we flew under a cloud, the plane jolted as if it were falling, and I grabbed the first handhold I could find, a strut at the side of the cabin. Frederick beside me was as serene as ever, and we flew on, until under the next cloud it happened again. Then we came out into the blue, and to my astonishment Frederick let go of the controls and folded his arms.

"Look," he said. "How well she flies herself!"

We flew, and still we flew, I never knew how far. Everything was strange and new and beautiful. The air that came in through the cabin window was fresh and sweet. The changing colors of the earth with its woods and fields, and the ponds with wind streaks on them, all were different from anything I had imagined. As the shadows from the hedges became long saw-toothed markings on the grass, we came back and landed. Tired but delighted, I sat quietly as we drove home. I thought of what I had done. I flew that flight over and over again, around and under the clouds, picturing again the things I had seen, the very same things that I see every day, but all made into a pattern, lovely and gay. I saw the city, transformed. The high buildings made across the landscape an irregular line of tiny facets that caught the light, and the water towers shone like mother-of-pearl. I saw the elaborate contour lines of the farm land, and the little groups of trees and houses, and large, lonely woods. Everything was a pattern, not one new world, but an infinite number . . . worlds changing as we watched, as the light changed, as the clouds moved and the sun sank in the west.

The day was Saturday, October 5, 1946, more than a decade ago.

I shall never forget that Saturday, for that day fate committed me to an adventure, which is still an adventure, and one which I have never regretted. Life became lively. I woke now to the morning sunshine, and for a magic moment, in half awakeness, I lay still, solving as slowly as I could the secret of my pleasure. It was a delicious game, for I knew that I already knew the answer, as I know in a dream that I am only dreaming. Each morning I re-flew the last flight, and planned those to come.

From that day on, I missed no opportunity to go to the airport and fly. Saturdays were reinstated to their old position as the week's most desirable afternoon. On other afternoons, too, I would watch the sky and the clouds. Once in a while, I would wander into Frederick's office, hoping that he would finish work a little early. We flew often during those autumn weeks, for the weather was fine, and I was eager. From that day on, we talked flying, Frederick and I. We talked and talked, and a flood of communication was re-established between us. I pestered him with questions, as if to make up for lost time. I read the Civil Aeronautics technical manuals on the theory of flight, engines, navigation and weather, and stories and novels about pilots and their airplanes. I soon learned the language of the airmen, and was delighted at the vigorous and picturesque expressions. Some of them were lifted straight from the world of the sea, but others were quite new, and tailored to fit the new element. I listened to the talk of the people who sat on the benches at the airport . . . pleasant, friendly people who never tired of aircraft and "hangar flying." I learned much from them. At first, as a beginner should, I listened. I was like a child, admiring from a distance, full of envy. Later, when I had gained experience, I found myself accepted on equal terms by them. I understood the strength of the bond among airmen, who know what it is like to be alone above the world.

That Saturday, the fear that had dogged me all those months, everywhere I went, the unleavened misery that was like a lump in my throat, began to move away, out of my life. The more I learned, the less I feared. It had been a dread built and fostered by ignorance, and it cannot ever come back. It had yielded, in the balance book of my experience, nothing but debit, and there were no compensations. That Saturday the balance book began to show credit entries of many and unpredictable sorts. No day has passed since then that has not been flavored, for me, by my thoughts of the sky and of aircraft. I have found infinite delight and fun, and more delight, in the air during these thirteen years, more fun than I ever thought I could find in life. And if the condiments thus sprinkled on my daily round have been, once in a long while, a little too strong for my taste, and I have had cause to wish I were safely back on the ground, even that, to my everlasting astonishment, gets entered on the credit side. It is entered there as a job done to the best of one's ability, without panic . . . a crisis faced and handled, something learned about the airplane and myself, confidence gained.

I delighted more and more in our flights. Nothing happened to mar the pleasure; nothing spoiled the dream, the exquisite fun, of being in the air. And during those days the possibility first occurred to me that I might even learn to fly myself. I was thinking such thoughts, half afraid that the dream would end, when one evening we came in over the airport and saw far below a strange plane, low-winged and silver.

"That's one to watch," said Frederick. "We'll keep well out of his way."

I saw the plane approach, and then go round the field again. It made several such attempts, as if the pilot were unsure of his ability to make a landing. Every time, just before it touched, it went up again.

We circled, to see what it would do. Then at last we saw it land, swerve, and smash itself hard against the runway bank. It bounced, shivered, and lay still, half across the track, and slowly a great cloud rose over it. Horrified, I stared down, watching the cloud, dreading to see in it the inevitable red gleam of fire. Oh, God, I thought, it might be my husband down there. Some poor woman's husband . . . dead . . . or dazed and bloody, about to burn. This is what can happen! We have to land, right there beside it. Will they pull them out, before we get there? I saw men with fire extinguishers coming from the hangar, running and milling around. The cloud began to settle. It was no fire, just dust. Then with calm assurance a voice broke in beside me. "Don't worry, I'm sure they're all right." But I was sick and giddy as we lost altitude. Frederick knows so much and I so little, I told myself. If he says so, they'll be all right. I kept on repeating it, without belief . . . a phrase to hang one's hopes on, to keep up one's courage.

Down at last, we rushed past the wreck and on past the gathering crowd. We climbed out and walked back. There, alone in the center of a group of pilots and mechanics, stood a magnificent Negro, elegantly dressed and bearded. He was unhurt and laughing; his hands waved about and his eyes moved back and forth around the circle of astonished onlookers, but beneath his nonchalance was defense and embarrassment. He was on his way home from the South, where he had bought the plane that day, army surplus stock. He had stopped for gas. It was the twenty-third plane he had cracked up. He had to get home, he said; he was a doctor and his patients needed him, so he accepted the offer of a lift into town. He walked deliberately away and did not look back. He left no address, nor did we ever see him again. They pulled the wreck into the nearest ditch, and left it there, and it rusted in the winter rains. In spring the tall weeds grew up and covered it, and it was forgotten.

Every time we flew during those weeks we learned something. Frederick handled the Chief expertly now, and I became more and more interested in our new sport, although only as a passenger. To add to my pleasure, I was not airsick, even on bumpy days when the Chief, seemingly deliberately, stepped into holes in the sky, one after another. For a person who has been as seasick as I, this discovery was a profound delight!

Then one quiet evening, late in November, Frederick, without warning, let go of the controls and indicated by a gesture that I should take them. We were heading north from the airport, along the road to Roxboro, where it passes over a causeway between two ponds.

"Fly along the road," he said, "and relax! And if you don't like your situation, just let go. I don't mind what you do, as long as we have plenty of altitude."

I knew what the rudder pedals and the wheel were for, and what they did to the airplane, for I had read about these things and asked all sorts of questions. And it certainly looked easy enough when Frederick was doing it. The plane flew straight and level when he had the controls, and it did almost as well by itself. Here goes, I thought, and swallowed hard. I'll be very careful, and hold on tight. But when I took hold of the wheel, we were instantly neither straight nor level. It was not as easy as it looked. I held on tighter, and we began to climb, for, my muscles tense, I pulled back on the wheel. And the right wing was lower than the left as I dragged the wheel over, as with my legs stiff and my feet jittering on the rudder pedals, I worked to keep the road ahead of me, where I could see it over the nose. So, crabbing with the rudder, and in a peculiar nose-high slip, we danced and sidled like a skittish pony up the Roxboro road. It was a curious maneuver, compounded of errors. I could never do it quite like that again, for it was a perfect example of mishandling, a prime demonstration of what not to do. But after all, it flew, and I was myself in charge of the controls of an airplane! Overwhelmed with delight and amazement that this should ever happen to me, I worked and struggled. This, I decided then and there, was something which I must find out how to do. I was middle-aged, and set in my ways, and all that, but this, without doubt, was for me!

From that day my mind was made up: I must learn to fly. Frederick said yes, and in the bank was a reserve, built out of years of teaching medical students, which could be used. But I was forty-four years old and my hair was very grey. The students I saw at the airport were all young, and only one of them was a woman. What about the tales of reflexes and old age? What of motivation and the learning process? Above all, how would I harden my shell against the inevitable "She's too old to fly" argument, either expressed or implied? Back and forth I considered it, every day.

Every time Frederick went to fly, I was along, and I learned, from him and from my own efforts, more and more. I began to sense the amount of pressure necessary on the controls, so that I could fly straight, or make turns. I became more and more sure of what I wanted, but although George, the instructor, was often at the airport when we were there, I could not make up my mind to ask him. I made excuses to myself. I would do it next time. Just supposing he said no, what would I do? That couldn't happen! He would surely give me a trial, after all I'm going to pay for it. But there was always the doubt, the horrid suspicion, that perhaps I *was* too old.

I have good reason to remember that Thanksgiving Day, and so has my friend Alice. It was clear and windy, and I longed intensely to fly. I never looked at the sky with such deep desire, and there I was in charge of a house full of children and an oven full of turkey. I considered, and then I did something I had never done before. I called Alice; could my kids go over and spend an hour or two, playing with hers? Deceitfully, shamefully, I took the children *and* the half-cooked turkey, and before she could protest, the turkey was in her oven! I don't think I have ever been quite forgiven. Children? Why, of course. We all do that for each other, and with pleasure. But not a turkey. The responsibility is too great. Anything but that! I understand how she felt, and I understood even then. The turkey was perfect, done to a turn, and we ate it together. I offer Alice here and now my most humble apologies. I have no excuse. I just couldn't help it.

Turkey and children were forgotten as Frederick and I took off. A wild gale tossed us about as we worked and pushed our way upwind from the airport. The trees and houses danced back and forth under the wing strut as I watched. We would cross a road, and it would catch up with us again. Two steps forward, one step back, we fought the wind. Eventually we turned homeward and now the wind hurried us along so that the earth rushed past us, and too soon we were over the airport, and then we were down. We pushed the plane into the hangar where the wind could not harm it, and we went into the office. George greeted us pleasantly as we came in, looking up from his seat on the sofa, and his half-eaten turkey sandwich.

"Do you think," I asked him, "that you could teach me to fly?"

He stopped eating and looked me up and down. There was a long pause. Then, gently but firmly, as if I had doubted his ability to instruct, he said, "Of course. I could teach a mule to fly!"

I got to know George very well, and he never, never in any way made me feel that I was too old. Years later, I reminded him of his remark about the mule. "I didn't think," he said, "that you would ever make it." George was always patient and forgiving of my mistakes, and ready to answer my questions. I could not have found a better teacher, and I owe him a great deal.

So, on the Saturday after Thanksgiving, at four o'clock, I took my first official flying lesson. I bought a logbook in which to record my flying hours, my dual time signed by a rated flight instructor. It lay, with the other student logs, in a pile on the office desk. I hoped, oh, how I hoped, that I would not be inept with the controls. I had, I figured, a little experience with the Chief, which should help me at the start, and perhaps I would be able to solo in eight hours, which is considered about average. The instructor, I knew, had complete authority to allow me to solo any time. He could, if he found me competent, get out of the plane after only one hour, or he could stay with me and never let me go alone. I hoped I would not disgrace Frederick or myself; how I hoped I had not attempted the impossible!

CHAPTER 2

The horizon, which spread out before me as the plane rose from the ground, was only a small part of an immense area of interest that opened for me when I began to fly. This delighted me, and it still does. I discovered that the ability to handle the controls of an airplane is only one of the skills of a pilot. A pilot must be, in a special way, an expert weatherman; he must know how to make use of the information supplied by the weather stations, and he must be able (this comes only with experience in the air) to estimate the virulence of a black cloud that lies across his path, or the nature of a silvery line in the distance . . . fog, perhaps? . . . so that he may outwit the enemy. During my earth-bound years, I would look up and assume that the clear skies or the rain clouds which were part of my life that day must also be part of the lives of my friends, at the seashore, perhaps, or far away in some distant city. But in flight, when a mile or two pass by every minute, the weather changes are astonishing in their rapidity. Fifteen minutes after take-off, made in the gloom under a heavy overcast, there is light on the horizon, pale blue-green light, and soon I am borne gloriously out into sunshine, and my spirits rise as I gain altitude. Or, we are rushing toward a cloud bank, and I must push the nose down to creep under it, hoping to find space to squeeze below, hating the prospect of turning back.

And the pilot must be navigator, too. He must know how to find his way around in the sky; how to use his compass, watch and radio, and check them against the landmarks on his course. Only a few of the pilots who fly, as we do, for fun, learn the difficult technique of flying by instruments; most of us fly "contact" by Visual Flight Rules. We use the earth below as our reference for level flight, and each pilot has his own special method, his own way of navigating. Some depend largely on radio aids, and some prefer to use the compass and visual checkpoints. I wanted to learn all of this. And the theory of flight, even in its simplest form, was quite new to me. I found out about angles of attack, and parasite drag, and Phugoid oscillations, and what makes an airplane stall and spin. I found that airplanes have individuality, so that each one is different, even from its twin. Engines, too, are special, and every propeller, finished as it is by hand, has its own peculiarities. And I discovered, unbelievably, that —compounded of a subtle blend of oil, grease, gasoline, dope and paint—each airplane has its own rich, heart-warming smell.

Diligently, I studied the traffic rules of the air. I learned who may fly what kinds of plane, and where and when; who has the right of way, and many other details; a very elaborate code of behavior. And I learned the regulations concerning the upkeep of airplanes, their registration and airworthiness certification. Airworthiness: a word borrowed from the sailor, which still hits me with a little blast of pleasure each time I hear it. An honest, forthright word; a word for a well-constructed, well-kept ship for either sea or air, one able to withstand the buffet-tings; one which will take you where you want to go, even across the world.

Finding out so many things kept me busy and happy when I was not flying, but I had, in those early days, a more important project. I had not forgotten, for the memory was only a few weeks old, the miseries of my fears of the unknown. So I set myself to find out, as exactly and scientifically as I could, why accidents happen to light planes. I read everything available, all the analy-ses, treatises, books and articles I could lay my hands on, and this is what I found: fatal accidents can be avoided, except for a few, a very few cases. There are two main causes. First there is the pilot, usually newly licensed, who spins his plane into the ground as he circles low over his girl-friend's home. A spin starts out of a careless, skidding turn, and there is no time to recover from it before the end. Or, the pilot who pushes the weather instead of turning back, and sticks his nose into a stuffed (or an unstuffed) cloud, followed by the inevitable loss of control, and the deadly spiral, faster and faster until the plane hits the mountainside, or the wings are torn off. These account for most of them.

The non-fatal accidents, when the airplane is smashed with little damage to the pilot, usually occur on take-offs or landings, and again are almost always caused by carelessness or poor judgment; pilot error is the term that is used. And what happens, people ask me, if the engine fails? Well, of course they do fail, but rarely. And when they do, you must land, from wherever you happen to be at the time. But you can always glide slowly down into a pasture or even a wood. Keep your head, fly your plane and don't let it spin; there's no hurry, pull it up gently just before you touch and let it drop in, at the slowest possible speed, even into the treetops if you have no choice. Just another landing! The impact is much less severe than with a car, for a plane is so much lighter. Do it well, with good judgment, and you won't get badly hurt, even though the plane may be torn to pieces.

And yet, accidents happen, and people believe that flying is dangerous. I soon learned, as I watched and listened, some of the reasons why. It was in winter, during my lessons, that two men took off from a nearby airport, before dawn. One was a student, the father of two small sons, and the other was his instructor; three weeks later they were found in a wood only a few miles away. The plane was turned back toward home, and had cut a swathe through the branches before it crashed. Probably they died at once, but perhaps they lived for a while, lying there helpless. No one knows. They had flown for less than ten minutes in that terrible dawn, before they changed their minds, and tried to get back, and crashed. The weatherman could have warned them, but he was not asked; heavy squalls and thunderstorms were forecast for the area.

It was about that time, too, that I first met Ichabod Crane. He was invited to a breakfast flight by the owner of the red and yellow Piper Cruiser. He had never flown before. He exploded with enthusiasm, and by the time we all reached home again, he had bought the Piper.

Once in a while, the pilots at our airport would meet early on a Sunday morning, and fly somewhere, to eat and talk. The companionship is pleasant, and beginners can learn a lot that way, watching and listening. Frederick and I, who had so little experience of cross-country work, were glad to go along. That morning, it was still almost dark when we reached the airport, and the hangar lights were blazing. The planes, stacked very close together, were being untangled. Presently they were out, sitting on the wet grass, each one in a magic circle, where their owners, walking around them for a pre-flight check, had left footprints in the dew. I shivered a little, partly from the excitement of the airplanes and the trip, and partly because of the cold dawn. We planned to go to the mountains, and I wished I had brought a heavy coat. Then an instructor came out of the office. "Flight canceled," he announced. "The weather bureau reports fog in the mountain valleys." But we were hungry, and had struggled out of warm beds, and the planes were all out and ready. People stirred restlessly. "Meet you all at Ashton, for ham and eggs!" yelled a voice, and a plane started and taxied out. Ashton, a tiny bedraggled one-runway place, even smaller than ours, was only twenty miles way. No fog there! Hardly far enough to take off, before it is time to land again. But fun, and good practice, too. We would go, and so would everyone else. One by one propellers started to whirr, and one by one the planes taxied out, in a long, lurching, staggering line. As each one came to the end of the runway it revved up its engine, turned and rushed off, becoming graceful as it became airborne. Frederick and I, in our Aeronca Chief, were eager to get going, but we were almost last in line. The Cessna ahead of us balked; it had a dead battery. At last they got it started, and we followed it, and took off. For a few minutes we were alone in the dawn sky, and then, as we peered ahead, we saw the landing field at Ashton, now a nest of huge orderly wasps. Several circled above while they waited their turn to land, and there were two rows of planes on the ground, facing each other, and the rows became longer as more planes came in, landing in the narrow strip between them. I felt secretly glad that I was not in charge, for it was no place to swerve, or ground-loop, or even bounce. Frederick, I knew, would handle it, and of course he did.

Next to the road that ran alongside the airport was a little café, now utterly disorganized. Caught unprepared by the mass arrival from the skies, the proprietor dashed back and forth. Pilots and their friends milled around, too, looking for hot drinks. Supplies were rushed out from town, tables were set up on trestles, and in a short time we all sat down to plates of country ham and eggs, biscuits and coffee. I found myself sitting near a lanky young man, whose hands and feet seemed strangely outside the sphere of his influence. His eyes were set deep in his bony face, and they glinted through a wild fringe of hair. He talked loudly and incoherently as he ate ham and eggs and more ham and eggs. He was Ichabod Crane, I decided, whose feet (and hands) were like shovels. I soon discovered, to my pleasure, that he knew little or nothing about aircraft, even less than I did. Soon everyone around knew it, too, so they started telling him extravagant tales. About the airplane which had hovered back and forth over the airstrip before it landed; how, low over a river in head winds strong enough to keep the plane stationary, a pilot had turned fisherman! And all sorts of wonderful stories of the good old days of barnstorming. Ichabod became crazy with eagerness, and full of plans. He must learn to fly. He would solo within a week. More eggs. I think he ate six. How could he get a student license? Where could he buy a plane?

Presently we were finished, and again we all rose

up into the sky, and soon we were back home. There, after we had gassed our Chief, and put it safely in the hangar, we learned that Ichabod had bought the Piper Cruiser, and was already taking his first lesson. From that day on, he was to be found at the airport every day, fussing, begging, arguing and cajoling. When could he solo? Why not today? He could handle the Piper, his own plane. "Too fast and too far down the runway," the instructor told him. "It isn't safe to land, if you do that. There isn't room. You'll overshoot. You must go round." Rules that had been beaten into me, over and over again. "If you don't land on the first third of the runway, go round! Three times, four times round, there's no disgrace in that. *But don't land and overshoot!*" At last Ichabod soloed, and he was a happy man. He flew, day after day, while we held our breath. He would come in fast and high, and just in time he would push the throttle and up he would go, over the road and round the pattern again. We would sit in the office, watching him through the big windows, shaking our heads.

Then the inevitable happened. Even faster and higher than usual, we saw him coming. Halfway along the runway he was still six feet off the ground. On and on, toward the trees, the wires and the highway, he floated blissfully along. The wheels touched, too late now to go round again, and oh! too late to stop! Ichabod knew, in that moment, only one thing to do, and he did it. He stamped on the brakes. The tail rose up as the nose went down, and with a tearing crash the propeller hit the gravel, sending splinters in all directions! For a long moment it hesitated, and then, slowly but surely, over on its back went the Piper Cruiser as we rushed out to help. It came to rest under the wires, broken and ruined, and inside, hanging upside down in his seatbelt, hands and feet flapping as usual, was Ichabod, unhurt. We cut the magneto switches and pulled him out, and he stood there a moment. "Well," he said, "George was right. I should've gone round. A thousand-dollar landing!" It was several years before I saw him again. We had based our Stinson at the big airport at Chapel Hill, and one hot summer afternoon a Cruiser came in. The pilot was Ichabod, and he had two passengers with him. They strolled around the hangar, and drank soft drinks, and gassed the plane. Presently the two climbed into the back seat, and we moved away into the shade and watched. Ichabod, on the ramp, pulled the propeller, and as sometimes happens with airplane engines when they are hot, the Cruiser did not start. He worked and worked without result. Desperately he was swinging the Cruiser, arms and legs and propeller going round like a whirling dervish. Finally, two of us got up, and moved over lazily in the heat to see if we could help. Ichabod was drenched with sweat. There were no chocks under the wheels, the throttle was fully open, there was no one in control in the cockpit, no one to hold the brakes, and the two passengers, their cheeks full of gum, were contentedly waiting their doom in the rear seat! How could they know? An airplane at full open throttle needs only a single tiny spark, an explosion in one cylinder, and the thing goes berserk. With no one to close the throttle or hold the brakes, and no chocks to hold the wheels, the propeller pulls the airplane forward in a great circle, and once started, it cannot be stopped. First, the plane charges the man in front of it, and chews him to pieces with the propeller, and next, it rushes about with increasing speed, looking for more victims. Often it chops up other aircraft on the concrete apron, or it tears into the hangar wall. If its path is clear, it will even take itself off, rise up and fly, perhaps until the gasoline is exhausted. Such accidents, which are unnecessary, are rather frequent. The amount of force that is packed behind the turning prop is hard to believe. And Ichabod? I think that in his ignorance he had managed to flood the hot engine with gasoline, and that was why it wouldn't start. Three people might have died there, that afternoon. After a while we got the Cruiser going, and they took off. I have not seen Ichabod since. I heard a story that he got lost and crash-landed the Cruiser. Perhaps he doesn't fly any more. It isn't his game.

When Ichabod soloed, I had only a few hours of dual time, and I knew very well that I was not ready to fly alone. I wondered what it was like, and whether I envied him, and I was not sure. I wanted to solo, of course, but I wanted, with all my heart, to become a skillful pilot, and the solo flight is only a beginning. I was in no special hurry, as long as I was learning and gaining experience every time I flew. I was busy, too, with other matters, and finding time for lessons was not easy. Fortunately the evenings, the last hour or two before sunset, are the best time of the day, for then the wind drops and the air is quiet. When storms are abroad, with their centers pushing east or north, so that one air mass is being displaced by another, the winds may be strong and persist even into the night, but in settled weather the late afternoons are generally quiet, even if at midday the branches wave outside my window, and the lazy buzzards, spiraling upward, outline the invisible pillars of air, the elevators on which they ride.

Light aircraft in flight, or on the ground, are profoundly affected by wind. Fierce squall winds, the ones which precede the summer thundershowers, are much to be dreaded. They can turn an airplane over on its back, or break tie-down ropes and pile planes into each other on the hangar ramp, and do much damage. An attempted landing, under these conditions, may be thwarted by a sudden and complete reversal of wind direction, and, on the ground, taxiing may be impossible. Even little gusts —too weak, you think, to do anything but bend the grasses on the runway's edge—will push a small plane around. Sideswiping as you approach for a landing, a gust can tilt a wing so that a beginner lands on one wheel and swerves out of control; or it can lift you just when you think you are down, and then let go so that the plane falls hard onto the ground. Or, a few hundred feet up, it can blow so that, instead of the rectangular ground track the instructor told you to fly, all you can manage is something shaped like a baseball diamond, or even a piece of pie. And when he points out to you what you have done, you can hardly believe it. That much drift hardly seems possible! Ordinary turbulence is not dangerous when one is airborne, but for a student, trying desperately to maintain the attitude of the nose and wings, the bumps of a summer day will much increase his difficulties. Gradually, after hours of experience, the pilot learns to expect and anticipate the effects of wind on the plane. Then a windy day becomes a challenge, compensation becomes rapid, and it is hard to remember those early times when even a light breeze added so much to one's troubles.

So, in those days, I began to watch the clouds and the wind very eagerly, and to study the local weather changes, conditions I had lived with for many years, but had never noticed before with other than casual interest. The mornings are calm, for then the air is shrunken and dense from the coolness of the night, and morning would be ideal lesson time, but for the pressure of the day's work ahead. Later, during the hours when the sun warms the ground, the hot air, rising in columns, causes local pressure differences, with turbulence and gusty surface winds; these usually increase till midafternoon, and then, often with surprising speed, they fade out as the sinking sun allows the air to cool again. I would plan for the evening hour for my lessons. Sometimes, if the wind still blew, George and I would sit in the office and talk, and I would pester him with endless questions. And there were wasted days, when I did not even go to the airport, for the sky was cluttered up with low-hanging clouds; or days when I could not escape from my work. These were the hardest.

On three afternoons every week during term, we have classes in the laboratory, which do not end until five o'clock. However, the students often finished their work early, and teaching would be over for the day. Then I'd run to my car, and drive fast to the airport. But there were agonizing days; days when the sky was blue and the trees waved their branches with ever-diminishing vigor, and the students stayed and stayed and the minutes dragged. Usually, I stayed, too, but once in a while, I remember, the urge would be too strong for me, and with a furtive aspect I would get my coat, and creep down the back stairs and out, telling myself to assuage my conscience that I had done more than my share of the teaching that day; that I would do a better job next time if I relaxed; that one or more of the staff had been away from the lab anyhow for an hour or two. Still feeling desperately guilty, I scurried out to the little airport, and everything but flying was forgotten.

The lessons, George explained to me, began with work high in the air, at altitudes which were safe for recoveries from deliberate or accidental stalls or spins. Straight and level flight, turns, climbs, glides, and last but not least, stalls and recoveries from them. I learned that in flying engines may "quit," but wings "stall"; that is, the flow of air over the wing is, for various reasons, pulled loose from its moorings on the wing surface. The suction or "lift" is lost, and the wing won't fly. Once you know how, recovery is simple. Push forward on the stick as if to dive for the earth, and as the speed increases, the wings are in business once more. So, one must work on stalls, as the Civil Aeronautics Manual says, "out of all anticipated flight attitudes." Turn . . . and stall! Climb . . . and stall! Glide . . . and stall! Again and again, until the student develops a built-in stall-recovery system, guaranteed automatic! Only then is it safe for him to work at lower altitudes, to learn to fly close around airports, and finally to learn the techniques of take-offs and landings. After six lessons, I could recognize an approaching stall, and I knew what to do about it. I had even done some spins, which are just exaggerated stalls. I hoped I would soon begin landing practice. Six lessons, three whole hours of flying time, officially entered in my logbook and signed by George.

I remember the day of my seventh lesson. I found George waiting in the office, and together we walked out to where the Aeronca trainer plane, tandem-seated with dual controls, was facing the runway. We spoke of the last lesson and its problems. I glanced at the scattered groups of boys by the railings, and they stared back at me. Did they envy me, I wondered, for the race I was to run, in a few minutes now, out into space? We checked over the plane, and got in and fastened the safety belts. Over the little stones on the runway we rushed, stick forward until the tail was up, gathering speed, rudders working to keep the nose straight, and then I felt the sudden lightness and lift as the wheels left the ground.

The stick moves back and the plane starts to climb, smoothly up and over the trees. The delicate controls respond now to every touch, the heavy drag of the ground is forgotten, and the world widens. Below, two cows in the meadow are touched by the passing shadow of the plane. Up we go, to safety and freedom and space. The altimeter reads four hundred feet now, and I remember that this is a lesson. The traffic rules require a left turn here, before we leave the pattern, and it must be a careful turn. We are still near the ground, so it should be a level, not a climbing turn. Put her nose down for straight and level flight and glance past the wing tip for a land-mark so that you don't turn too far, and then bank her carefully. Don't pull back on the stick to keep away from the earth; that is the way to stall, and a stall is the way to disaster. She turns smoothly and I right her, and start climbing again, out of the traffic pattern now, heading for the well-known fields over which the hard part of the lesson will take place. I make climbing turns, first left then right, nose up, one wing tip hugging the horizon, with just enough rudder pressure to keep turning. Re-member, a touch of *right* rudder for a left climbing turn, to keep her steady against the pull of the propeller. Sweetly, slowly, she turns, back and forth, up and up. The world is mine.

I hear George's voice behind me. "At three thousand feet, do a spin to the left. She's all yours." The spell is broken and the world forgotten. Now, I must make the effort, the struggle to co-ordinate brain and limbs and senses to an unfamiliar design. Can I make her do it? Almost three thousand feet now, and a wave of panic flows over me. I open the window a crack and feel the rush of cool air. Can I do it? I know what to do, of course I do; haven't I done four spins already; I can do another today;

of course I can. This is what I do, in this order; there's nothing to it. First, look carefully all around and below, for other traffic. Close the throttle, pull back on the stick, and then press hard on the left rudder, and she'll head sideways and down, and into the spin. And I know what to do then, for I have been taught, and so I can get her out of the spin, and if I can't, the instructor can. Ah, George . . . I glance around and see him sitting behind me, hands and feet off the controls. He grins. "Go ahead! Relax!" Not even a jellyfish could relax now, and someday I'll tell him so, but the spin must be done. *I* chose to take flying lessons, and I will do this spin. I will! So . . . everything in order, stop the roar of the engine, hard back on the stick, and give her full left rudder. The plane rears up, leans over, and the nose falls. The earth with its fields, the tiny houses and the highway, lies far below and in front of me now, as into the spin we go. The tail is up, the nose down, and the wings rotate slowly around. I see the highway disappear and then come into view again. I feel myself one with the plane, relaxed at last. Now, to recover . . . rudder pressure off, stick slightly forward and back again. Check the air-speed indicator and don't let her dive too fast. The rotation stops and she gathers speed. Back with the stick until the nose comes up; open the throttle and enjoy the rough, friendly motor noise; and now the earth and the plane are in their proper places once more. "Did you get me out of that?" I asked. And George replied, "You did it all yourself."

Then I hear his order, "Back home we go, straight

and level." Yes, sir, very gladly, if I knew which way to go, but now I'm afraid I'm lost. The landscape looks very strange, and I know it is a disgrace to ask the way. After a glance at the compass, I gently turned the plane around. Heading due north, it told me, and I started north from the airport, away from the town. I made a one-eighty degree turn and as we swung to the south I recognized with joy the two ponds and the causeway on the road. My troubles for this day were surely over. I wriggled and slid down in my seat, for I knew she would fly herself now, and George was always telling me to relax. Dammit. I sat up, for the engine had stopped! Think, think hard. Is this the crisis they say is always round the corner? Establish a normal glide, at sixty miles an hour, and then try to see what is to be done. There's a fine field over that way, but you cannot stretch a glide. Can we reach it? Phrase after phrase, complete from the Civil Aeronautics Manual, sprang to my mind. Why must this happen to us now? "We'll have to make an emergency landing. Which way is the wind?" His voice is quiet and steady, and as I turn I see that the throttle is fully closed. O.K., sir, it was all a trick; you did it. We'll make a landing right there, in that field of winter wheat, even in the pigpen. I don't care. *You'll* have to fly her out. You caught me napping that time, just as you hoped, and I thought it was the real thing. Down we go, with a gliding turn into the wind. Yes, we can make it, and not too low over the trees. And as the bright green wheat plants separate into a myriad individuals, I feel the throttle pushed forward, and we sail up again. The chickens scatter. Over the barn we go, safe and headed for home.

I circle the airport, get into the traffic pattern, and idle the motor as we lose altitude; turn again and steer her for the narrow runway, over the wires beside the road. Steady her against the little gusts of wind, which lurk near the trees to catch the unwary. There's my car, in the parking lot. Glide down, stick gently back to raise the nose to a stall as she settles, and once more the wheels bump over the gravel. I taxi her to the hangar, undo my safety belt and climb out. I walk into the office as steadily as I can. I record the flight in my logbook, the instructor signs it, and I arrange to come back at the same time tomorrow. Three and a half hours' official time now. Oh, but I'm tired! I feel for my keys as I walk to the car. It runs home, without conscious direction from me, for I . . . I am still above the world, spinning and turning. Twenty-three and a half hours to wait, much too long.

All the next day, through the routine of lectures, conferences, lunch and labs, my thoughts drew me toward the window, and out to the trees and the sky beyond. All day the sky was blue, but the branches of the trees moved around; they swayed back and forth, with their leaves bright and changing from green to silver as the wind pushed at them, and their undersurfaces flashed as they turned up into the light, and settled into place again. No luck today, I decided. George didn't take beginners out in a wind like that. Then I turned away from the window to help a student who stood beside me with a test tube in his hand, and for a few moments I forgot. The next time I looked, the trees were quiet. The wind must be dying, I thought, and then . . . wham, the branches whiplashed back on themselves as a gust caught them. Put flying out of your mind, I told myself; it's no good today. But when the students had gone and the lab was empty, I drove out to the airport to see if I could find George, and there he was, feet on the counter in the office. "Glad you came," he said. "I want to talk to you." So now, I thought, is he fed up with me, with my slowness and my persistent questions? Will I have to look for another instructor? "Up till now," he said, "you have been average, maybe a bit better, I'd say. Your air work is good, and you got hold of spins sooner than I thought you would. From now on . . ." and he told me at length about the techniques of take-offs, and of flying around the landing field, or pattern flying, and of landings, and especially how to salvage a bungled one, and what was safe to do, and what was not. This is the way you do it. Glide, steadily and straight, toward the chosen landing place, and when you are at the right height above the ground, break the glide by pulling the nose of the plane slowly up. This is the flare-out; pull back on the stick (not too fast and not too slow) so that the nose rises gradually, just to the right angle. Then, just as the plane slows and the wings stall, the tail must touch the earth, and just at that moment the wheels must touch, too, and the stick must be just at the end of its travel, all the way back! The three-point landing! Simple, isn't it?

"Above all," he told me, "remember that everyone has his troubles, some with take-offs and some with landings, so don't get discouraged." I have often wondered since whether George, who was so wise in the ways of students, had already, by some sixth sense, foreseen what was to happen.

At the next lesson, we started flying the pattern. Take-off, climb, turn, climb, level off, glide, turn, glide, flare out and land. Over and over again we did it. Take-offs, at first, were wild, as I lurched from one side of the narrow runway to the other, riding the rudders, over-controlling, so that the swerves increased until, at last, the plane flew, staggering off the ground. But after a few attempts I found out how much rudder pressure was required to keep it running in a straight line, and then I could take off, safely and smoothly. I could fly it all the way round, except for the landing. Round and round we went, for another try. Sometimes I started the flare-out too late, and the wheels hit the ground, and we soared up in a mighty bounce; George took the controls before we stalled, or we would have dropped suddenly and perhaps broken the landing gear. Next time round, I leveled off, too high and too soon; George took over before we stalled, twelve feet above the runway. Hours of it! I began to hate the ground as I glided toward it; a mixture of hate and fear of the transition stage, the moment between earth and air, flying yet not flying. "Relax!" said George. But every time, as the ground closed in on me, I stiffened on the controls. More hours, at the same game. "Aren't you tired?" George asked me. "Aren't you bored?"

I replied. Patiently, he explained my errors, and the next time round he explained them again. He never said a harsh word, nor ever raised his voice. At home in the evenings, Frederick listened with sympathy as I poured out my tales of woe, and I felt better. Landings were a challenge to be met, another technique, and I had learned so much already, in time I would certainly find out how to do them. And I did, too. At last, I leveled off at the right moment, and the three wheels touched and stayed on the ground. But it must have been just luck, for at the next one I leaped like a grasshopper. "Get that stick back!" said George for the fiftieth time, "and keep it back!" Then one day he gave me a handful of forms, official-looking documents, and I filled them in, got my medical certificate, which the Civil Aeronautics Administration requires of all pilots, and obtained my student license. When George was sure that I was safe, he would sign it, with his name and the number of his Flight Instructor's rating, and I could solo. He was the judge of how many hours I needed, hours flown dual, with him in the seat behind me. Students have been known to solo after three or four hours' instruction, or as many as twenty-four. And some people never solo. I put my license carefully in my wallet, and hoped. I would solo soon, I promised myself. But that very evening I reached a new low, for, when the lesson ended without a single decent landing, and we walked together from the plane to the office, George said, almost to himself, in a puzzled, sad voice, "Surely it ought to come soon!" That evening, restless and exasperated, I walked up and down the road outside our house, fighting with myself. And at the next session, two landings were good, and two were not bad, and only three required immediate rescue work. The next time better yet, and I went home contented, and promptly started to fret. If I went on like that, I'd have to solo. How would it feel, to get up there by myself? Did I want to do such a thing? Of course I did, desperately; I wanted to be in the sky, and free and alone. But what sort of thing was it, for an ordinary woman to do? Those landings meant that one day George would get out from his seat behind me, and I would be on my own. Next time, tense again, I flew the plane into the ground and bounced. Then I relaxed; George wouldn't get out today. So then I did better again, and then, with thoughts of solo, I stiffened . . . and you can't land an airplane that way. So it went on. I had shamefully many dual hours now, and one evening, on my way home, with my car almost empty of gasoline, I turned into a tiny filling station within sight of the hangar. An old man, slowly chewing his cud, filled the tank.

"You be the woman that takes lessons up there, bain't you?" He pointed over his shoulder. "Some of the fellows was talking about you, said as how you was too old to fly!" I drove home angry, determined as never before that I would not quit. I'd show them! I'd find out how to do those landings! Those fellows! Probably the ones with no manners, who took off just underneath us today and balked my landing, all against the rules. Too old? Indeed, no; they were too young, that was the trouble. So, as I flew the pattern, I thought of those boys, and while I raged at them my landings were smooth, much better than they had ever been.

"Always carry your student license with you," said George, "and remember she'll climb much faster when you are alone, so don't get too high or you'll overshoot the runway. If you *are* too high, go round again; there's no disgrace in that. And come out as early as you can tomorrow."

Tomorrow came and I drove out, just as I had done so many times before. Suppressed excitement was deep down inside me; why did nothing look different? George and the airplane, take-off, pattern and land, and again. Would he stop me as I taxied, undo his belt and step out? What would it feel like? Not this time . . . and we took off again. It was getting near sunset now, and no breeze stirred. The wind sock drooped, flaccid on its high pole. I saw the new moon, a tiny frail curve of light, high above me. This time? I had about given up the idea as I turned and stopped at the runway's end. And then I felt a movement behind me, and George was standing on the grass, leaning in through the open door, buckling the belt across the seat he had left.

"Three times round the field," he said, "unless I stop you. You'll do fine. Good luck! Go ahead!" No last-minute instructions, to be half heard and promptly forgotten. George was wise. I turned the plane so that it headed due south as before, looked straight ahead down the runway, firmly refused to consider my situation, and pushed the throttle forward. How she ran, and oh! how lightly and gaily she rose into the air, now thick and still in the cool evening. She'd never felt like that before. I saw the moon above me. Straight out I rose, and turned, and as I glanced behind me, I saw that there was no one there! My heart missed a beat. I knew now, with all the certainty that was in me, that I was alone in the sky, and that I, only I, could get me down! Now I knew how it felt to solo. Again, I pushed my thoughts aside. Almost as if I could catch them in my hand, I gathered them up and put them into a corner. I would attend to them later; there was no time now. I wanted them, oh, so much, but not now. They interfered with my business, and I was very busy and they must wait, they *must* get out of my way. I was high enough already. Level off or you'll overshoot, just as George warned. Do your job, I kept repeating to myself, don't enjoy this and don't be afraid, don't be anything but just a mechanical device, part of the plane. The thing I am doing, consider its implications later, in an armchair, and not now. And the luxury of sensation, that must come later, too. Nose down, glide and aim straight; a good approach makes for a good landing, it looked all right to me, and there I was, down, and there was George, standing beside the runway and waving me on. Twice more round as the sun set, and then I taxied in and cut the engine. George was there, opening the door and shaking my hand, people crowding, congratulatory and smiling. I walked steadily into the office, and George signed my student license and my logbook, "First solo, fifteen minutes." Only after I was home and supper was over, did I sit down and allow my thoughts to come out of their corner.

Does what I have done today have the aura, I asked myself, with which it is, by tradition, surrounded? Consider it from the practical point of view, from the outlook of a person learning a new skill, any skill. It is only a stage in the learning process, a proof that, under carefully chosen conditions, the student knows how to push the stick, rudders and throttle to control the airplane. He has been taught the rudiments of swimming, and now he is thrown, irrevocably, into the pond. So of course he swims, but with stiff, mechanical movements, the responses to carefully worded orders delivered to his limbs by his brain cells. If the engine were to fail during the solo flight, what then? I remembered how often George, behind me, would cut the throttle and make me glide, turn and almost land. Sometimes there was no choice; sometimes a rough ploughed field or a weedy pasture. What sort of a job would I have done, I wondered, if this had happened? I had never experienced such a thing, so how could I tell? Would I be able to handle myself, and the airplane? All my life I had avoided such situations; I knew nothing of my instinctive actions at a critical moment. That evening, I wondered about it. Later, not so very much later, I was to find the answer to that question.

I had no illusions. I did not think that I knew how to fly. I knew that in the hours after solo, the beginner, free now to wander by himself in the sky, gradually finds relaxation and self-reliance as he accumulates his hours, the thirty hours or so that he must have before he can attempt the flight test for his private license. The "Private";

every student's goal. Permission to fly whenever and wherever he wishes, for the rest of his life, and take passengers with him.

As I sat by the fire, thinking of all that had happened to me that day, I knew that I had passed a milestone, and that a new world had come within my reach. I knew that the solo flight, for all its insignificance in the learning process, is, as tradition makes it, a memorable one. From then on, I would fly alone, and on that flight I had discovered that the sky is lonely. To me, this was unexpected. I realized it suddenly, at the moment of seeing the empty seat behind me as I turned. And this loneliness has never left me, through all my thousands of hours. Sometimes it grows until it is almost unendurable, and then again it may be only a whisper in my ear; mostly it is to be welcomed and treasured, but sometimes to be feared. It is a loneliness that can make me laugh with delight, or yell and scream with utter abandon. There's no one there to be outraged and run for help, believing you to have gone mad. No one to tell on you! Then there is dreadful loneliness when you are lost, or with a coughing engine and a passenger who trusts you. I think it is this loneliness which pulls, with such strange and urgent power, at those who have found the need to be in the sky. The complete alone-ness after take-off . . . the sharp and absolute break in the continuity of communication. No explorer in deep jungle, no sailor out of sight of land, is as suddenly torn out of reach as is a pilot, alone in a small airplane, six feet off the runway. That day I was sure, with all my heart, that I could never, of my own will, stop flying!

CHAPTER 3

The landings of my first solo flight were good ones, smooth and neat and satisfactory, and I was happy about them. And I had soloed, and I had thus proved myself to myself, and to my friends. The critical point of the battle was passed, and now there remained a tidying-up period. I knew very well that there was much to be done, but that evening I was contented and tired, and I slept a heavy, dreamless sleep.

For the next few days when I went out, George, who

was always ready to help, would fly with me for a few times round the field. Then I would be familiar with the conditions for the day. From the ground, it is often not possible to anticipate a slight cross wind and drift, or a down draft over the trees beyond the end of the runway, conditions which make the feel of pattern flying, especially the final approach, different each day. I was glad to have him there, and glad when he got out, and I was on my own. Then my day's work would begin. Round and round the field I would go, take-off, pattern, landing; taxi back to the runway end and do it all over again. "Circuits and bumps," the English call it. If I did a good three-point landing, I would hope to repeat it, but usually I did not, and I would decide on the nature of my error, and go back and try not to do it again. Sometimes I was the only student flying, and George would sit watching from the window of the office. On other days, he would be teaching in another plane, and there would be other students in the air, each working out his own problems. Sometimes three or four lightplanes would be in the pattern at once, carefully watchful to keep out of each other's way. Aeroncas are very slow, so they never overtake anything, but other planes would pass me on my way round, and land ahead of me; or someone would come in too high and miss a landing, to go round again and thus change the order of our procession. Or a plane would arrive from a cross-country trip, take its place and land in turn, and taxi back to the hangar; or one would come out, take off, and disappear into the blue. And whether George was flying or whether he was not, I could feel his critical eye upon me, watching my landings. And oh! how I would bounce!

It was during these days that I found, to my own surprise, the beginnings of a certain resistance within me. I dawdled at home before I started my car. I would wander to the garden and pull a few harmless weeds from among the bean rows, and then drive slowly along the familiar road. I even lingered in my office when teaching was over. And I did some dreadful landings, when the good training I had had came to my rescue, and saved me from serious trouble. It was at this time, too, that I first dreamed a strange fantasy, a dream which came back many times in almost the same form. I would arrive at the airport, undo my personal zipper fastening, and take out my heart. I wrapped it carefully in a transparent plastic bag, and set it on the stove in the office, to keep warm. There, bubbling and sloshing in bright red blood, it beat steadily inside the bag, while I flew. I would re-place it before I went home.

Why were my landings so bad? Why, I puzzled, was I so tense? Could it be, I asked myself very privately, that I was scared? Scared to fly, after all I knew about what not to do, and how not to do it? I tried to sort out my feelings, and tell myself that my problems were normal, for who, other than a moron, would not be scared, a very little bit scared, to be up there all alone? Surely it was ordinary prudence to be scared. It was the price I paid for what I got (and it was strictly payable in ad-vance)! If it were understood, and put into words and admitted . . . Yes, all right I am scared . . . then why couldn't I relax and do better landings? I argued that a person who deep inside himself had no such feelings, must be a dangerous pilot, insensitive, lacking normal braking mechanisms within him. But in spite of all my efforts, I would get out of the airplane after a half hour's work in the sky, and my knees would be weak and wobbly, and my fingers, when I tried to write in my logbook on the office desk, refused to obey me. I watched the other beginners, but I saw no signs of any trouble. To me, they looked entirely unreactive, even phlegmatic.

On a grey, cold Saturday afternoon, about a week after my first solo flight, the students gathered at the airport, a little flock of us. George got us started, one by one. He would keep a watch over us, while he flew with a newcomer, who had not yet soloed. A traffic cop came out to fly his new silver Cessna, and work at spot landings for his Private license flight test. These are difficult maneuvers, for the engine must be throttled back as the plane flies down wind, and the turns and altitude so gauged that after a cross-wind glide and a turn into the runway, the plane is neither too high nor too low, but is in position to land on, or very near to, a designated spot. I listened while George spoke. "You can turn short, if you are low; or make it long if you are high, even an S-turn. Play your turns. A wide pattern, that's the secret." Such niceties, such elegance, were almost beyond my understanding. I could not think in those terms, I who was glad enough to get down anywhere, so long as it was somewhere near the end of the strip! Presently the cop turned to me. "She flies real good," he said with a pleasant smile. "Will you ride with me when I get my license?" And there was a stranger, a heavy-set man with gloves and a hat, not the flat eye-shading cap of the pilot, but a town hat. Presently the hat, and George, climbed into a green Taylorcraft, and they flew twice around the field. Then George got out and the T-craft took off; the hat was solo.

The two Aeroncas squatted there, waiting. I went over to my favorite, the Old Lady, I called her. There were butterflies inside me for sure, a whole crowd of them. My frankness to myself had made them worse, not better, as I had hoped. The words had defined the truth, and it was written down, indelible, never to be unsaid. I was scared! All right, so I was scared. I would fly this afternoon anyway, and not let the people out here find out about it, especially George. I pre-flight checked the airplane, gas and oil, controls in order, tires and the fastening of the cowling, and then I sat inside and waited, while George was talking with his student, a very young man, tall and eager. As George talked he used his hands, demonstrating the turns and banks, steep and shallow ones, nose down on corners, showing how it should be done. Then he came over to me. "Off?" he called. "Off!" I cried, and he pulled the propeller a few times round. "Contact!" and "Contact!" I replied as I clicked the magneto switch into the "On" position, and the Old Lady was alive and ready to go. Then the other Aeronca burst into activity, and I led the way as we taxied out, and took off. Up and around. And my landing? I leveled off high in the air and almost stalled. Oh, yes, and George was up there with a ringside seat, watching me. Well, at any rate I wouldn't do that again, so next time I flew it wham into the ground, and bounced up, and when I finally stayed on the runway and turned onto the grass, I turned and saw the Cessna, so elegant and trim, gliding in behind me with never a break in the continuity of the movement. Following it was the green T-craft; good, too. At the next one, I was much too high, and I didn't even try to land. In disgust, I pushed the throttle forward and went up again. Still no good. I was forcing myself, tense and anxious. What would George think? George, the master of the flying art, who made his airplane a part of him. United, they were a dancer, bending and swaying in rhythmic movements, effortlessly; or a big bird, wing-tip fingers spread out for the banked turn, an aileron pressed down to catch the slipstream and lift the wing. Was George, I wondered, born that way, or did he have to learn to fly? Did he ever struggle with the stick and rudders? I hardly thought so. It must have come naturally, that smooth, gentle control, yet control with full authority. George and the airplane flew as one, but they flew where *he* wanted to go, exactly and precisely. Like a child, I watched and longed to do the thing that looked so easy. I hated my clumsy experiments and my jerky rough movements, and I was sorry for the airplane that I maltreated so, and for myself. Had I better give up for the day, call it quits and go home? Oh, well, one more try, and as I landed and turned I saw ahead of me the other Aeronca, waiting in the grass beside the runway. They are talking, I thought; George is

telling him some things. I was about to squeeze past
them and take off, when the door opened, and George
jumped out and ran toward me, waving his arms. How
most unusual! I'd never seen him do that before! I
braced myself, more tense than ever, for the long overdue
bawling out I was sure was mine. Would he be angry or
sarcastic, or disappointed after all the trouble he had taken
with me? What would he say? He ran and came around
from behind, circling the airplane in which I sat, and as
he passed by the open cockpit window he said, "Relax!"
and with hardly a pause in his stride he ran back, and
in a moment he was away, and airborne. Astonishment,
relief and then amusement filled me. He understood, and
I went off after him, laughing a little and gaining confidence, and my landing was better. How can he tell? I
thought. How does he know so much? Next time round,
I felt fine. I pulled back on the stick and held it in position, and when the wheels touched, they stayed. Eventually, I promised myself, I would know all about these
things, like George. After that I did better, and a few days
and some solo hours later I asked for permission to leave
the pattern and go exploring. George said yes. "Only for
God's sake don't get lost," he said. "Keep the airport in
sight, or go along a road. And work! You have plenty
to do. You can practice figure eights, or S-turns across a
road. Remember the wind direction. Have a good time!"
We had talked about these figures, and I knew what they
entailed. Like so many maneuvers, they are exercises in
turns, one way and then the other, combined with compensation for wind effects, so that the track of the air-

plane over the ground makes an even figure, an eight or a letter S, not an elongated, lopsided or misshapen affair. The wind pushes you away and you have to turn short and steep, or it pushes you back and you must fly out into it before you start a shallow turn; always it nudges you, with persistent and invisible urging, and always you try at these practice times, to circumvent it. Even on a quiet day the wind effects are quite recognizable, and on a rough one, as I learned later, it takes a lot of concentration to prevent yourself from being blown out of position.

So off I went, alone in the sky, alone in charge of an airplane. I set my course north, on the main road from town. The lessons had been over this farmland; it was open country with plenty of fields where a landing could be made if necessary. I knew it well. The school and the church, the river, the two ponds and the causeway, and a long double row of tall poplars, all in turn passed below my wing. The poplars, at evening, would make shadows on the grass like a picket fence, laid out flat. The palm of my hand where it gripped the stick was moist with sweat, so I deliberately let go, and wiped it on my blue jeans, and then I took my feet off the rudders and wiggled my stiff toes. What should I do to relax? Where should I go? I was free at last to do what I pleased, and what was I doing anyway, up here in the sky? Below my wing strut, the cars moved along the road. Some, going my way, were slowly overtaken as I flew, and others, going toward town, passed quickly. There was a flash of light as one of them caught the sun, and it darted under me, a yellow car, yellow as the wing strut itself. It was in an extra hurry, that one, and I turned the Aeronca to see if I could find it again, and there it was, ahead of me, chasing merrily along. A little car painted bright yellow, down there with someone driving it, and a little airplane above, painted bright yellow, too. The car was moving fast, so that only gradually I caught up and passed over it, while my air-speed indicator showed eighty miles an hour. But I was in no hurry at all. I would have helped the unknown driver when, at a bend in the road, he slowed behind a truck; get on, I would say, I can see the road ahead, it's all clear for a mile at least, you are quite safe to pass. But he waited, and I, watching, saw the truck swing out onto the straight section of the highway, and saw the car, delicately pushing its nose out and out, trying to pass . . . and I saw it drawn in again quickly, as the horns of a snail might be, back into place. A car swept past them both, heading north, and again the yellow one poked out a feeler, and this time, bold, it turned and moved on, passing the truck. Liberated, it sped on the long straight road, and I chased it. From my place, a thousand feet up, I could see what he could never see, and go, where he could not go. It was I, the liberated one, who turned and banked and twisted; I who flew over wires and fences, rivers and houses, where there are no roads, no footpaths even. Practice S-turns, George had said, and suddenly I found a game. I crossed the highway directly over the yellow car, at right angles to it, and flew out, over the fields. Then I turned carefully back, found my car, and crossed again, just over it. S-turns across a road, with a moving target to complicate life. This was a fine game, and I squealed with joy. I must turn just steeply enough to keep in position; if the car got ahead, I dived to catch up with it, or if it lagged I pulled up to slow my speed until it was there again. Over it, and back over it, free in the air a thousand feet up, I forgot myself completely. A woman, I thought, and a grandmother; a reasonable person with a professional status, sedate and middle-aged, and at the thought I squealed again. I followed the car until the houses began to crowd together under me, and it stopped behind several others and waited. The first traffic light. I left it, and presently I went back to the airport. "Did you have fun?" asked George. "Yes, I did," I told him, but I didn't tell him what I had been doing.

After that, I found all sorts of unexpected things to do and an unlimited amount of pleasure, in a half hour after work, an airplane, and the evening sky. Sometimes I climbed up high to four or even five thousand feet, where the wind that came into the cabin was chilly, and found its way into my heavy jacket, so that I shivered and closed the window, and throttling the engine to idling speed, I made long, steady, spiral glides, down and down to the airport, a postage stamp far below. Sometimes I stayed very low and close to the earth, and I would follow the course of a brook, winding with it through the fields and woods, downstream until it met and joined another, and together they flowed on, toward the sea. Even when it is hidden under trees, water will show telltale glints of reflected light; a river, wiggling like a snake, brought memories of geography lessons in school, of sand that piles up on the inside of a bend, so that the water flows farther out, and a sand bar forms, growing longer and thinner all the time. The river writhes, more and more strained, until the sand bar, by now a piece of the forest, breaks at the weakest point and a new channel is born. The old channel, the oxbow, dries up, and the process begins again. I could see it as I had never seen it before, every stage from the very early wiggles to the almost complete ones, ready to break off, it seemed, at the next flood. Sometimes I would trace streams toward their origins until they eluded me, and in this way I discovered that the local watershed runs right through the campus, and I look out on it from my office window. To the north and east, the waterflow, however it winds and curves and wanders, eventually drains into the Neuse, and out to sea. To the western side, the flow is into the huge valley of the Haw River. The next time the rain poured down, and I couldn't fly, I went out and paddled around in raincoat and umbrella, tracing the water flowing into the culverts and away. There I stood, with each foot in a puddle; this water, around my right foot, may at last reach the sea through Albemarle Sound and on past the famous dunes at Kitty Hawk, and past Kill Devil Hill. And the water around my left foot is fated for a long trek to the port of Wilmington, past the docks and the ships, and out to sea.

On clear evenings, from two thousand feet above the airport, one can look over a vast saucer of fields and woods, perhaps forty miles in any direction. There are often several tufts of smoke to be seen. These vary little with the source, but greatly with the wind. They act as wind indicators, and can be valuable on cross-country trips. Sometimes a smoke tuft lies short and low along the earth, flat down like the ears of an angry cat. Sometimes they go straight up, and sometimes, in the quiet dusk, they drift slowly across the world, close to the ground, hugging the hollows and making long, long streaks. Maybe three or four of them will lie parallel, fading into the far hills. As the sun sinks, a twinkling light will show beneath a smoke tuft. A farmer burning trash in a field, or a tragedy, a house on fire? I never can resist the urge to go and see, and so, one day, wandering in the evening sky, I turned aside on my way home to look at a big one. It was a farmhouse, ablaze in a grove of huge oaks. Flames poured out of the windows. I could see people leading cattle and horses from the barns, and the road was blocked with cars. There was no water near, and I saw the flames leap high as I circled, carefully avoiding the rising column of hot air. The oaks began to flame. Round and round I turned in a gentle bank till the roof fell in with a sudden burst of fire. I saw the burning embers rise into the air, over the tops of the oaks. As they scattered and fell back, I came to my senses.

The sun had gone down, the hills were already very dark, and my haven, the airport, was not in sight. No lights on the airplane or the runways, no alternate airport I could reach before dark. The gloom pressed down tight upon me. I started down the road, and those well-known curves were never so long. I dived slightly, to squeeze a few more miles out of the air-speed indicator. At last I saw the runway and got into the pattern, low, stirring in my seat as I relaxed. But it was too low. The trees near the end of the strip must be cleared, and the failing light made judgment difficult. So I got up a bit. Suddenly the runway was there and I was high above it. With the strip under me, and to one side, there was only one thing to do; go round and start the approach again. That meant five more minutes and it was already almost dark. I opened the throttle fully and cut the corners to save time. Skidding corners low down is bad, so I flew with deliberate attention to detail. I checked the fastening of the safety belt; it was tight. I made a low pattern and a long, straight approach with a little power between the dark shadows that I knew were an apple orchard and a bunch of tulip trees, and this time I came down to a smooth landing. I taxied slowly to the hangar, while I composed my face and tried to quiet my thumping heart. "Yes, I was out a bit longer than I intended!"

My solo hours accumulated slowly. Always, on those evening flights I hated to turn back, but now I watched carefully as the sun lowered itself toward the horizon, and I turned with time to spare before dark. Then I landed and went home to supper. More and more as I flew I relaxed, and more and more, I had fun. And after a flight, on my way home, I would find that the trials and irritations of the day had shrunk to a reasonable size, that I was suddenly and ravenously hungry, and that the world, for me, was a very pleasant place.

And while the solo hours piled up, there were weekends to look forward to, for Frederick and I, every fine

Saturday, would fly radially out from our home base, exploring our new world. Toward the mountains, or the sea, wherever the mood took us, we were free to go. We would make our plans the evening before. I took my pack of charts and sorted from among them the ones we would need, and certain extras adjacent to the course, which might be useful in an emergency. I used the sectional charts, made by the Coast and Geodetic Survey for aviation use. Lovely things that cost only a quarter each, they tell a pilot just about everything he wants to know about the ground beneath him. I spread them out on the floor of the living room, placed together in the correct positions, and I drew the course, from point of departure to destination, as a straight red line. During a flight of a few hours, one may travel over several charts, so I arranged and folded them suitably, and then I sat and contemplated the red line. I noted with anticipation the landmarks (check-points, we call them) on the way, the time which should elapse from take-off before we passed over them, and especially the airports which were near our course. These appear on the chart as circles, with their altitude, length of runway and other pertinent information printed alongside. In some parts of the country there are very few circles, and in other parts, around the big cities, they are clustered so closely together that on the map they overlap each other. They vary, from the great hard-surfaced municipal fields, with many runways, airliners and traffic-control towers, to rough turf strips, privately owned, with maybe a right-of-way, or even cattle feeding on the landing area, and often trees, wires or other obstructions on the approaches.

With but few exceptions, we are free to land at the airport of our choice. If I like, I may sandwich myself between the DC-6s at Washington National, and the tower (radio contact is essential here, and at most of the large fields) will treat me right and land me in my turn. After all, I pay taxes, don't I? Often, however, I prefer the tiny grass strips, where I forget about airliners and radio, and concentrate on putting my plane on the ground exactly where I want it, at the slowest safe speed; the elegant "short field landing." The techniques are different, but the feeling, as the wheels touch down, is the same; those designated areas are something very special.

So, Frederick and I would decide upon our circle, find it, fly over it and land there. Then we would take a look around and come back home. Every flight taught us something new. I learned, very soon, that an airport clearly marked on the chart may require an experienced eye to find it on the ground below. A grass runway can hide in a mess of small fields and woodland so that, although you may fly many times around where you know it must be, you cannot find it. The map shows it there, between the highway and the river. Look for a cross, the St. Patrick sort, made by two intersecting runways, or a couple of airplanes lined up at the edge of a wood, or some flat wide sheds, which might be hangars. Or an airplane, taking off or landing, or its shadow, flitting over the trees. There's nothing there, nothing that anyone could possibly land on. Well, you think, maybe it's been closed, and ploughed up. This time, it doesn't matter. But you don't like it, and you feel insecure. After all, you might have wanted it, very badly. At that moment, something catches your attention, and there it is, clear as anything, and you wonder how you could have been so stupid! Once you have seen it, it is unforgettable, and with time, a strange sixth sense grows upon a pilot, correlated from all his past experience, so that he can find, with no trouble at all, those tiny, important circles. Flying cross country, then, I always try to check the circles with the landmarks. The sky seems less lonely, as one of them slides below. I like to be aware of the distance to the nearest one, and the direction, often indicated by a railroad or highway. The fact that I know it is there, and do not need it, is a matter for satisfaction, though it is, of course, routine. But sometimes things get tight. A thunderstorm . . . which way to go? Unexpected engine trouble . . . can we make it? Darkness, and a head wind, harder than we figured on, or gas running low? . . . There's one answer . . . the nearest circle. Look for it, find it, get down, and be thankful.

After a few solo hours in the vicinity of his home base, the student pilot must learn the rudiments of cross-country flying, and before he can obtain his private license he must fly, solo, with his instructor's permission, and land at airports a certain minimum distance away; and a certain minimum number of hours must be spent on such trips. All this must be recorded in the logbook and signed by the instructor, the student, and someone at each airport where a landing was made. I looked forward immensely to these expeditions, and I was very pleased and proud when I first had permission from George to leave the home airport and go to Chapel Hill and shoot landings. Twenty miles away at least, out of sight except from high up on a clear day, and I was allowed, even encouraged, to go there all alone in charge of an airplane. I would make those landings good ones; I would be relaxed yet alert, like the man in the textbook, and ready for anything.

The runways there, which later I came to know so well, are long and wide, all grass. There, there is no need for the meticulously planned spot landings of home, for no one could overshoot that enormous place. An airplane can sit down safely, more or less anywhere, wherever the final approach and glide leads it. I felt wealthy in the possession of so fine a prairie.

I flew around in the pattern several times to check the traffic and at last I was ready to land. I saw the wind sock on the hangar roof, and chose the runway into the gentle breeze, and descended. The tufts of grass hurried past me as I flared out. But at the instant of the stall, I was too high, and, too late, I recognized it. The controls went limp and I dropped, perhaps only eighteen inches, but still not good. The grass was tall and dense, and the hard heads of the flowering onions beat upon the wheels as I taxied. Off I went again, and up and around the field for another approach. This time when I lined up, I was slightly off the center of the runway. A smooth, steady glide took me well over the boundary of the airport and down. I pulled the stick gradually back, with the wings level and the nose up, and this time the grass was just where I wanted it. When the stick was back to the limits of its travel, the stall broke clean; this would be a good one. Suddenly, the world exploded. The airplane shivered and shook, and the engine missed beats. Things flew out in every direction, whirring wildly. My heart turned over and a great lump formed in my throat, and I held on to the stick, hard back, while I reached for the magneto switch. But then all was quiet. The propeller turned evenly again, and the wings seemed whole and unhurt; and so was I. I sat there for a few moments, and then I undid my safety belt, and pushing the door open against the blast of the propeller, I got out and walked around the plane to see what had happened. I found two small brown bodies in the grass, and blood stains and feathers on a strut. I had landed on a covey of quail! They say every landing is an adventure.

A few days later, I played hookey. I took off in the late morning to make the long solo cross-country flight required by the Civil Aeronautics people. I wasn't troubled about it. I had flown that way with Frederick, and once seen from above, the shape of the land cannot be forgotten. On the ground, I can get totally lost among a couple of city blocks; yet in the air once I have flown a course I know where I am. No land ever looks like any other, no two towns or streams are to be confused. The contours stamp themselves upon my mind, indelibly, not to be erased. So I flew in blue and perfect weather, to

Eastonville, where I landed, gassed up and waited to pay the boy who filled the tank.

He moved toward the Aeronca, expecting to swing the propeller for me. I pulled out my logbook. "Please will you sign this?" I said. The boy, already puzzled at my small airplane, blue jeans and grey hair, was now bewildered. "Yes," I said, "I'm a student pilot on my cross-country." He scrawled his name in my logbook, started the plane and walked toward the office, scratching his head. Utterly contented, I flew on. I held the stick between my knees and folded my arms, and followed the railroad, a big double-track one leading to the town of my next stop. Why bother with a compass? Soon the mountains spread out on the horizon, tempting me to go on. Someday, another time I would go, but not today, and I landed again. Then into the home stretch, southeast, with no railroad, an ill-marked, sparsely inhabited land of rolling hills covered with pines. Compass course, one-twenty; this is the time to remember to believe your compass. Keep one-twenty, that's the way home. And in keeping the compass course, I forgot to fly straight and level, so that unaware of it, I eased back on the stick and climbed almost a thousand feet. Well, why not? I'm free and on my own, I can do as I like. Follow the compass. Climb some more, deliberately now and begin to look ahead for landmarks, for my watch says it is time. There it is, the lake with the two tall chimneys on the north bank, and that means home is only a few minutes away; four thousand feet now, and I took a careful look around and below me and kicked the Aeronca into a spin. Out, and into another, the other way. Was it more fun to start out on such a trip or to arrive back home? The full moon, a great orange cheese, rose as I slid past the apple orchard and over the wires. My flight was over.

Now at last I began to feel that the Private license was within my reach. I had met all the requirements, except for a few hours of solo time, and it was all entered in my log, to be presented to the examiner when I flew with him on my test flight. All sorts of different eights, spot landings, stalls, I had worked at them all. George flew with me on a check flight, and it was satisfactory. He would recommend me for my Private. So, my hours completed, I flew the Aeronca to Danford, with my log in my pocket, and a bunch of forms signed by George, to find the examiner. The office was crowded with people, and filled with the thick smoke of cigars, and I stood in the doorway, hesitating, and then I sat down on a bench in the sun and waited. Presently, a Cub circled the field and landed, and out of it came a fat boy and a tall, bald-headed man with confident, easy movements. He spoke to the boy as they walked toward us, and I saw the boy set his mouth tight, and roll his eyes, and shrug. The man, towering above me, held out his hand and smiled. "You want to ride with me?" he said. What nice people, I thought, these airmen are. What component is it, that makes for such ineffable quality? The examiner sat beside me on the bench and we talked of airplanes, weather and navigation.

"I couldn't give him his license," he said as he rose.

"His fifth attempt; and he almost snagged a chimney on his forced landing!"

Presently we were airborne, and I worked through all the well-known maneuvers. Specially, I thought, keep a good idea of direction and don't get lost.

"Get into a spin," he said, "and as soon as you are in it, get out. . . . O.K. . . . Now a forced landing. . . . Where will you go? Into that field? . . . Which way? . . . Into the wind? . . . That's low enough, no need to scare the chickens. Good! Where's the airport?"

"We're too low to see it," I replied. "But it's over that way!"

"Home then," he said, "and three times round the field. A wheel landing, a spot landing, and a slip." I had worked on these for hours. Wheel landings are fast, tail up and power on, for better control in a wind. The spot landing is to show judgment of altitude, in case of an engine failure. The slip? A nice trick of deliberate crossed controls, when the flight path is held by pressure on a rudder. That way, one can come in high and then lose altitude without diving and gaining speed, and then floating on and on, across the field. One can slip, safely, almost to the ground, and then level out and land, slowly and prettily on the shortest runway.

I did my best, but was it good enough? It wasn't very good. He smiled as we walked to the office. "You'll do," he said. "You are a bit rough on the controls, but you'll improve." So, following him into the office, I knew that I was now, and for the rest of my life, a

Private pilot. I had grown up. I waited, while he slowly typed a certificate, and handed it to me.

"Good luck!" he said, "and come and see us often. You'll get your permanent ticket from the CAA in a week or two."

CHAPTER 4

That evening we celebrated, for now at last we were both pilots, and for many hours, late into the night, we talked of flying. We asked ourselves, as we had done so many times before, what it was that we both enjoyed so much; and, as so often before, we found no real answer. We told each other how fortunate we were. The more we talked, and the more we speculated about the future, the greater became the possibilities of our new-found game. What did we want out of it? Just to get up into the sky, above the world? To go somewhere, wherever it might be? To meet the challenge of the weather, with its infinitely variable attacks? To achieve the graceful flight of the expert, gentle and smooth? To potter at the airport in the oil and grease, fussing with minor repairs? To get to know as much as possible about how an airplane works? To take our friends for rides . . . and perhaps to find among them one or two who feel as we do? All these things were ours.

So we talked for a long time, and presently we came to some conclusions. We were happy with the Chief, but we wanted a larger plane, faster and more powerful, one which would carry us and our friends, and even some suitcases. We had gained much experience during our cross-country travels, and we were ready for more. The strategy, we decided, was to sell the Chief, and buy a four-place airplane, a Stinson. It would cost a lot, as much as a luxury car, but (I think in spite of our discussion the decision was predestined) we could afford it. That is to say, we *would* afford it. And as to the sort of airplane we wanted, there was really nothing to discuss, for everyone was in agreement that we should buy a Stinson. So, before we slept that night, our minds were made up. A Stinson it would be; a well-built four-place plane, with plenty of power for its size; reluctant to stall, and almost impossible to spin; a forgiving airplane, pilots call it.

Soon afterwards, George and I went to bring it home. I had never seen a Stinson before, and I did not know what to expect. There on the ramp it waited for us, fat and red and shiny. And although that day was more than eleven years ago, I well remember how beautiful it looked to me, and how I drew in my breath at the realization that it was ours. It is still fat and red and shiny and even more beautiful, for it is decorated now with the memories of many flights and the fun of all those years.

That afternoon George flew it home, and with me beside him he took off and landed it, again and again. Then he would climb it high above the field, and stall it, and then down again. Suppertime came and went, and still we flew, getting the feel of it, enjoying the power and the smoothly elegant performance, the lovely slow landings. We played with it that evening as if we would never stop.

At the airport, we asked for advice: who would look after our new airplane? Mr. Randolph was the man, they told us. He knew Stinsons, inside and out, propeller spinner to tail-wheel assembly. If we could persuade him to undertake the upkeep of our beauty, we would be fortunate, for, we were given to understand, Mr. Randolph had nothing to learn. He was one of the old-timers, and though he no longer flew, he still worked on airplanes, and he dated his experience from the days of the barnstormers, when repairs were made on the spot, often with nothing but wire and nails. So one day we flew to the airport where he worked. I have often thought it was too bad that he was standing at the door of his shop just as we came in, for the landing was not one to be proud of. Perhaps, otherwise, things might have been different. Mr. Randolph had thick black hair and a tanned face with keen, twinkling eyes, brightened, I think, by his many thousands of hours in the air. He was a man of authority; a ponderous, slow-moving person. I pictured him, sitting by a fire on a cold winter evening, a drink by his side, telling tales of the good old days of long ago.

He led us into his office, through the hangar full of big aircraft which towered over us, and he gave us hot coffee. While we drank, he talked to a young man, and the young man answered him in a language I often could not understand, it was such an intricate mixture of technical and picturesque phrases. When Mr. Randolph turned to us and Frederick explained that we were beginners and in need of help, I felt how far we were from the ranks of the elite. We would put the Stinson in his care, if he would accept it. We wanted it kept in first-rate condition. Mr. Randolph-who-had-nothing-to-learn came outside with us and walked around our plane with the air of one who is used to bigger stuff, and the Stinson seemed to shrivel a little under his gaze. Anyway, he agreed to help us. It would need various adjustments, a coat of wax and polish, and this and that. He would keep it and work on it.

"Where did you learn to fly?" he asked Frederick suddenly. It turned out that he knew Connecticut well, much better than we did, and he had flown over it at treetop level many times. He filled our cups with more coffee while he talked of his many adventures, and managed to indicate what we knew already—that he had nothing to learn. I asked him boldly when the Stinson would be ready. Mr. Randolph couldn't say, for after all he was doing us a favor, and the work must be done during intervals between more important matters. Moreover, he would do the work himself, rather than trust it to his assistants. He would call us when it was ready and with that, we had to be satisfied.

For three weeks we stamped and fretted, and in the afternoons, like lost souls, we wandered out to the airport, where we would stand around and watch, and perhaps if we were lucky we would get a ride; or, even though we were at the low ebb of our financial tide, we would rent a plane for a half hour or so. Finally, we called Mr. Randolph. The carbureter, he told us, had failed to satisfy him, and he had sent it back to the factory. The Stinson was grounded. So we had to wait some more, and weeks later Mr. Randolph called to report that the carbureter had come back and he had installed it and that the plane was ready. How beautiful it looked! It gleamed in the sunshine and it leaped from the runway, a huge, powerful creature, an airplane I loved already, and longed to handle with relaxed elegance. I wanted to be expert, and I had so far to go. Now at least I could work, and learn. So once more I was at the airport every fine afternoon, practicing take-offs and landings, trying different techniques, flying round and round the field. With the whole great instrument panel in front of me, it seemed complicated to fly after the trainer plane, and immensely powerful. I worked at it, rejoicing. This was fun! I had about ten hours of Stinson time now, and about fifteen since my Private license.

Sunday was a clear and beautiful fall day, one of

the best. Our friends, Dick and Betty, had often said that they would like to fly with us, and so we planned it. When I telephoned them, I heard the excited shouts of the children. I went out early to practice. George helped me push the Stinson from the hangar, and I gassed and checked the fine, polished airplane, and got into it, happy and secure. I taxied to the extreme end of the runway, turning so that the tail almost swept the bushes. I headed northwest, over the pond and the highway, feeling the power of the big engine as, at full throttle for take-off, it pushed me back into my seat. Soon, I was at four hundred feet, and I looked behind me before I turned. Up to eight hundred feet, and then I came downwind in the familiar pattern, and landed. Then off again, and this time, just as I started the first turn, the roar of the engine stopped. Silence! Oh-my-God! Where's George? This is one of his tricks! He's down below. Remote control? No, this has happened to you and you must look after yourself. It's the real thing and in the worst possible place. Don't think of turning back, you're too low and you would only stall. Straight ahead it must be, even though there's nothing there but scrubby pines and small, rough fields. I see a herd of cattle in the biggest field. Cattle move, pines don't! Try carburetor heat. Switch magnetos—I read about that somewhere— left only, right only. No luck! Plan the approach. Get the trim tab back into landing position, but keep the nose down enough for safe speed. At any price avoid a stall! Switch gas tanks; maybe it's a clogged gas line. No! Well, I've got to land it, that's for sure. I'll do it, too;

I'll do a swell job. Doubts? Fears? I have none. I am concentrated to one aim, one direction, one purpose. I'm alive as never before. This is IT, and I'll do my best, nothing else counts. The black and white cows are there in front of me, and the field is very short and very uneven. Flaps down! Cows' tails up! They start to run. One last thing to try, I'll pump the throttle, I don't quite know why, it's just an idea. The engine gave a great, deafening roar! The nose came up as I pushed hard forward on the wheel, and reached to re-trim as I rushed close over the backs of the terrified animals. The noise echoed in my head. I saw an open pasture and I went there, not daring to climb, expecting silence again at any moment. I circled, listening, gaining altitude very slowly. The engine sounded smooth and healthy again, and soon I was high enough to get home.

There, waiting, were Dick and Betty and three children, and as I cut the throttle they ran forward eagerly to climb in. Frederick came, and I took him aside and spoke urgently. Such a sudden change of plans, on such a perfect day. They couldn't understand it. They were puzzled, even miffed, and the little girl cried; but there was no help for it. We all went home, thwarted and unhappy.

The days which followed were like ordinary days, but in the nights I would wake and relive those moments. "Oh-my-God!" I had said. As I lay awake, my mind raced; sparks flew like those from a smoldering fire re-kindled by the wind. In the quiet midnight the engine roared again as the cows waved their tufted tails.

Mr. Randolph offered to meet us at the airport the next afternoon. We were there as planned, but Mr. Randolph was ahead of us and had been and gone when we arrived. He left a message. There must have been a bit of dirt in the jet, he said, which had forced its way out when I pumped the throttle. That would account for it, and the airplane was fine and fit to fly. But a few days later, high in the air over the town, Frederick and I heard the silence as the engine cut once more. In an instant, he turned toward the airport and pumped the throttle; the engine started and we were home. This time, we were ready and waiting when Mr. Randolph arrived early, but the thing ran sweetly through all his tests.

He said, "There's nothing I can do."

"What about those filters in the gas lines?" I suggested, with the Stinson Operating Manual in my hand.

"I've done all I can," said Mr. Randolph as he walked to his car. "You don't have to fly if you don't want to!"

I flew . . . I had to . . . and for days the engine gave no hint of trouble. But it was different, for now I was afraid. I would take off and climb high over the airport, and circle there. As I swallowed to ease the dryness in my throat, the vibrations would alter a little inside my head, and I would take fright and pull the wheel around in a hurry to get back home. Then I would turn away again. I would discipline myself. Ten more minutes before landing, ten very long minutes.

I suppose it was about two weeks later that I went out to fly. I was in a bad way. I remember George filling the wing tanks with gas. My teeth chattered as I stood waiting, and his idle small talk was hard to bear.

"George," I said, trying not to seem eager. "Come with me! Give me a half-hour dual, will you?"

But George was repairing a broken window in the office, and I had to go alone. I looked at the Stinson. If you do have to quit, I begged, give me some altitude first, don't quit on the take-off! Out of the corner of my eye I saw the grasses move, and something wriggled behind the white fence, and separated to become the three fat beagle puppies that lived in the hut behind the hangar. They squirmed and wagged their way toward me as I stood under the wing. I scooped them up, all three in a bunch, a mass of friendly puppy. They reached up to lick my face, they crawled onto my shoulder, and rubbed their cold wet noses onto the skin of my neck. Puppy everywhere, fat and warm. I wanted to take them with me, those little symbols of serenity, but instead I put them back behind the fence, and I thought of them as I taxied out. I took off in a mechanical stiff-legged rush, over the wires and up. With every hundred feet I breathed a bit easier.

I had almost reached two thousand feet and turned north along the road, when the engine stopped; and this time it did not start again. There was the propeller, standing up in front of me, dead stick. I pumped the throttle and nothing happened. I pressed the starter button and the prop turned, but stopped again. A dead-stick landing it must be, on that tiny airstrip! Once more, gloriously, my fear left me. Unhurried, confident, I glided in a perfect pattern, quietly onto the runway. I braked to a stop and walked to the office, where George, his back to me, was painting the window frame. As I stood there, he turned. He saw me, and the plane sitting there in the middle of the runway.

"You did well!" was all he said, and together we pushed the Stinson into its shed and closed the door. It was then that my knees wobbled so much that I had to sit down.

We did not call Mr. Randolph. Instead, Frederick and I, with instruction books and Phillip's head screwdrivers and wrenches in our hands, set to work undoing filters, draining gasoline out of the tanks, gascolators and traps. We were desperate. George came by, bringing a stranger with him, and the stranger asked, "Have you drained the carbureter?" We unwound the safety wire on the big drain plug, which Mr. Randolph had so carefully put there, and unscrewed the plug. I held a Mason jar underneath it to catch the gas as it gushed out. There, in the gasoline, floated many little bits of newspaper, print still visible on them!

I never saw Mr. Randolph again, and I never knew whether anyone told him. I think he retired soon and left town. I had a hard time after that, for although I was sure without reasonable doubt that we had found our trouble, part of me was unable to believe it. It took me many hours in the air to get happy again. The stranger, Tom Dixon, took charge of our airplane now, and often I flew to his airport, where he was building a racing plane. He would look up from his job with a smile and a sideways glance of his deep blue eyes and ask, "Carbureter trouble?"

Gradually, with Dixon's help, we became familiar with the Stinson and its habits. Without spoken arrangement, it became my lot to take it and "go and ask Tom," and gradually I began to welcome the chance for the short cross-country trip, and the landing at another airport. Presently I flew solo with intense pleasure again, rejoicing in the lovely airplane and the freedom and expanse of the sky. As I flew home, an orange moon rose over the eastern hills, through haze turning to indigo as the sun went down, while the steady bite of the propeller bored through the thick air. The plane was like a huge beetle: beetle-like it changed course on a whim, to circle over a pond or visit a hillside before going down to a butter-smooth landing in the early autumn dusk. Those hours were unforgettable, delicious hours that made me young again. They took me back, after so long, to other enchanted moments: birds that started to sing with the dawn on a mountain meadow, or a long afternoon of skating on a pond, ending with the arrival of freshly baked bread, loaves to be torn apart in steaming hunks and gobbled under the bare willows on the bank. I found, in those evening flights, an enchantment such as I had never hoped to find again.

That fall was unusually fine, with many days of clear, cool weather. The afternoon thundershowers of summer were no longer a menace, and the forests blazed with color. We had flown several times to the mountains and to the seashore, but we had not yet explored to the north. We had a special reason, too, for going that way, for the family lived on the border between New York and Connecticut; and a big airport had only recently been built near by. How we had hated it; the bulldozers bringing ruin to the lovely country roads, pushing down the ancient stone walls, and tearing at the roots of the gigantic maples, many hundreds of them. We could land an airplane there now, on a flat, new runway, where bloodroot and hepaticas so lately flourished among the rocks. I had hated the bulldozers; but now I had to admit that I was glad for what they had done. With a guilty feeling in my heart, I condoned the slaughter of the maples!

We had often considered the possibility of a weekend with the family, but it seemed a big undertaking for us, who were such beginners. I had tried to do the impossible and imagine what it would be like, flying so far and over such great cities in our own airplane. Navigation might be difficult there, I thought as I studied the charts, for the railroads and roads are packed so closely that they merge into a dense network. There would be landmarks everywhere, a profusion of check-points, so many to choose from that they might be hard to identify. Airports? There were many of them. That would be fine. Big ones; and crowds of little ones on the outskirts of the cities, and many huge military fields, spewing up jets and other nuisances.

One Saturday morning I woke early, and the treetops were bright in the rising sun. Frederick was still asleep, so I lay quietly, plotting. After a while he stirred.

"Wake up!" I said. "Listen! If we left directly after breakfast we could be there for lunch *and* back for work on Monday."

He said, "What did you say?" but from the way in which he sat up, straight and suddenly, I knew that he had heard. But I had spoken with an assurance I did not really feel. Could we possibly find our way, the two of us, alone over that enormous country?

We called the Weather Bureau, and it was reporting CAVU (ceiling and visibility unlimited) all the way. We packed suitcases. We called the family: could they have us for the weekend, *if* we arrived? We planned, we said, to fly north, and we would call them from wherever we landed. No, they were not to worry; we were safe enough, and we might be there for lunch but we might not.

At the airport, for the first time in our flying history, we filed a Flight Plan. This is the way you do it: The pilot notifies the CAA, by telephone or radio, that he is taking off from (say) Cherokee; destination Currituck. He tells them the details of the proposed flight, the type of airplane, its identification number and its color; how much gas it carries, the route, the estimated time of take-off and of arrival. When he lands he must "close" his Flight Plan, for if he does not, the Civil Air Patrol, the police and even the military will soon be out, searching for him. There is no charge for this service, and when you are flying over desolate country, mountains or desert, it feels good to know that a search will be made for you if you don't check in! So, when a pilot arrives at his destination, he notifies the CAA. Sometimes, and this I specially enjoy, the tower will tell you, when you call for landing instructions, "Your flight plan is closed." I always hope it will be this way, for the sort of welcome-come-right-in feeling it gives me. We are expected; we are important (momentarily); they have been notified that we are coming, and now we have arrived as planned, on schedule. The authorities encourage the filing of Flight Plans, for in case of accident, search and rescue are much facilitated thereby; and, specially over inhospitable country, it would be foolhardy to fly without one. But there are, in the aviation game, two mistakes that cannot be excused, two unpardonable sins. When they are spoken of, the wise pilot will once more swear eternal vigilance, and mutter to himself, "Oh, let this never happen to me! Let me never run out of gas—or forget to close my Flight Plan!"

While Frederick was telephoning, I collected my charts and plotted the course. It would take us directly over the cities, and with good visibility we should see the coast and even the mountains far away to our left. So, we climbed in. How simple it seemed, how ordinary. Destination Westchester County Airport, almost five hundred miles away. And then we were airborne, and I noted the time. I settled myself to work: charts to be correlated with railroads, rivers and airports; wind drift to be corrected for. Check-point after check-point came and passed. Sometimes the chart told me—look quick, there's a stream down there, we should be over it; or I would see below me a road where it crossed a railroad, and I would hunt for it and find it on the chart. The pattern fitted like a jigsaw puzzle. The familiar country slid behind us, and the contour of the land became strange. There was the Roanoke River, with two bridges, far apart; the eastern one was the road bridge of U. S. 1; many times, I thought, I have driven over it, perhaps slowly behind a truck, smelling the exhaust gases that spoil the air; seeing the endless repetition of the billboards that plead with me, in a thousand ways, to open my wallet and buy; guessing how many miles I could make in the next hour; feeling tired and bored and irritable. I took a deep breath. In the sky ahead and just above us was a small cottony cloud, only one. I thought: Why had it no companions? Will others form around it, or is it the sole surviver of an early morning colony, hanging in the moist air above the river? Now we were over Virginia. After a stop for gas at Richmond we saw much water, and we flew along it until it turned at Washington, the great horseshoe of the Potomac. As we crossed it, we changed to a more easterly heading. Then in a few minutes we were over Baltimore, where the air, over the Bay, even high up, was tainted with excreta from the factories. Then we flew along the shore, carefully avoiding the forbidden airspace over the Aberdeen Proving Grounds. We saw the huge bridge spans crossing the Susquehanna at Havre de Grace; Philadelphia came out of the haze, and then Trenton and the towers of Princeton. And then we flew over crowded suburbs, the desolate New Jersey marshes, and we saw the skyline of Manhattan across the water. We were almost there. The sky was blue and a few white cirrus clouds were far above us.

Everything in turn, a perfect pattern. It seemed no time at all since we started, and there was the Hudson. Was it possible, I thought, that this was so easy? Too easy, almost. Would the last section of the puzzle, the airport, fit into place? The final, essential unit, like the keystone in the bridge. We came over the Palisades, losing altitude as we crossed the river. The Palisades are dwarfed from two thousand feet, but the river gains in stature. I could see far away the mighty sweep of water where it came in curves from between the hills at Bear Mountain Bridge, and it gleamed as it came. There were several strings of barges, making V-shaped wakes on the quiet surface. I looked around me carefully for other traffic. Now I could see the complicated and elaborate shore line of the Sound and Long Island in the distance. There, just ahead of us, was the airport, with its bright new runways close alongside the Croton Reservoir. We called the tower, and landed. We taxied a long, long way while they directed us and told us where we would find tie-down space. At last we turned onto the grass, into an unoccupied place in a row of small planes. At that moment, we turned to each other and with comical solemnity we shook hands and congratulated each other! "We did it!"

While I telephoned the family, Frederick called the gas truck. When the Stinson's tanks were filled, we did our arithmetic. We had used thirty-nine gallons of gasoline, and our flying time was four hours and four minutes. A trifle less than ten gallons in an hour, for a hundred and twenty-five miles, that's about twelve and a half miles to the gallon.

The family came very quickly to the airport. They inspected the Stinson with interest, but their enthusiasm was only moderate. But then they had not traveled, in comfort and in those few hours, a distance that was a long day's journey on a dreary highway; nor had they arrived as we had—clean and un-tired and fresh from a lovely trip in a lovely airplane, successfully flown.

Soon after our first trip to New York, the weather broke and it was winter. Flying days became less frequent. In the north, I am told that many planes are packed away by their owners to hibernate till spring; but here, dispersed throughout these months, there are usually some days that are warm and pleasant, days when it is good to get into the air. But winter flying has certain hazards, and that of ice is the worst. It attacks by devious means. Even a light coating of hoarfrost on a plane which has stayed out overnight will be enough to throw it so much out of balance that it may crash on the take-off. A layer of ice forming on the wings during flight can rapidly make a plane unmanageable. But much more frequent, and much harder to detect, is the growth of ice inside the carbureter, where it will accumulate and slowly strangle the engine. Maybe the pilot will notice the gradual loss of power and pull the control which heats the air as it mixes with the gasoline. Then the engine will cough once or twice and revive. But sometimes there is little, if any, warning, and engine failures are caused by such ice. The worst days are cold, damp ones; but rather mysteriously, even in warm weather under blue skies, conditions may be right for icing. A sort of feeling for it grows with the pilot's hours. He gets to know his engine, the beat and the quality of its roar, and the changes which may be of significance and those which are not.

Our Stinson's Franklin engine is well designed and does not ice readily; but one clear, sunny day, when we were high in the air on our way home from Charlottes- ville, Frederick grew tired of the controls, and I took over. Relaxed, I rested my hand lightly on the wheel while I checked the altitude and the tachometer setting. It was now my business to watch the instruments. Did the r.p.m. drop a little? The weight of my arm on the wheel would cause the plane to climb . . . I only needed to re-trim. But we seemed to be losing altitude rather than gaining it. Well, I guessed, it was a bit bumpy and you can't expect to stay straight and level all the time. Relax, let it fly itself. There's nothing wrong except that you haven't got the feel of it yet. The tachometer *was* losing r.p.m., a hundred, two hundred, and Frederick and I, our hands moving together, simultaneously, reached for the carbureter heat control and pulled it onto the ON position. The Franklin gasped as the ice floe in its guts broke loose, and the fuel passed freely into the mixing chamber again; it spluttered, coughed and then roared. The tachometer needle swung back into place and we had no more trouble.

The sun set very early now. The shortest day came and went, and Christmas was near. A week or ten days

passed without a visit to the airport. Over the supper
dishes or the ironing board, instead of woods and fields,
I would dive and turn, stall and spin. Sometimes I
deliberately worked on the technique of a maneuver, a
sort of dry run; but more often I flew in an imaginary
sky, where the sunlit towers of cities or shining mountains
lay beneath the fluffy cloud wracks of summer. Looking
out of the window at the grey coldness I knew was there,
I laughed at my secret fun and enjoyed myself. I could
fly, or I could not-fly. There was pleasure, either way,
and the choice was mine.

On the morning of Christmas Eve, the rush of last
minute shoppers was in full activity; and I, among them,
found a parking place at last. Locking the car door, I
smelled foul air and looked up. A still, cold day with a
heavy overcast, and the church with the great pillars
which is my landmark, was out of sight in the deep gloom.
The lights shone on the decorations on Main Street. Perhaps the smoke, caught under a warm layer, was unable
to move up and away; an inversion, the weather people
call it. On such days there is delight in not-flying, and
pleasure in not calling the Weather Bureau. "Yes, mam,"
he would answer me. "We're below VFR minimums
here, we have eight hundred and half a mile. We expect
some improvement, later today." Yes, I know, and the
yellow rotating light will be flashing from the control
tower, out at the airport, sending a warning message.
This is a day to stay on the ground, to relish the negative,
the not-flying.

Suddenly, as I stood on the street corner waiting for a chance to cross, the crowd stirred and people looked up. There was a roar, and above the street, almost as large as if it were in the hangar, came an airplane—a small one. I knew that sort, and I knew its reputation . . . not too good, in weather. Even against the dark sky, I could see the oil stains on the belly of the fuselage.

"He's buzzing!" said someone.

Oh, the poor fool, I thought, flying in this! I glanced around to find him a way out. North, south, everywhere, there was no light, nothing but impenetrable gloom. But who was I to fret? Was he, the unknown pilot, a man of experience, instrument-rated perhaps, with thousands of hours to his credit? Yet why so low over the city? Was he lost in that dreary mess, or was he happy, having fun? He will never know (or want, I hope) the deep sympathy I offered him from my place on the street corner. Lost, perhaps; with passengers who trust him; was he trying to identify the town and locate the airport? In that dark gloom, tearing up Main Street at two miles a minute, where did he go, while I suffered for him?

"Shall I gift-wrap them?" asked the girl in the shop, moments later. "Yes, please," I said. But my delight in not-flying was gone, because of the sight of that airplane, so low overhead. I'll never know where he landed, and he'll never know how he spoiled a shopper's peace of mind. Up there, so near and yet so far, he was in the dark sky on Christmas Eve. My thoughts were with him, many times that day.

That spring, Grandma reached her ninetieth birthday. For months beforehand, I had spent my spare moments working on an elaborate, pale pink Angora wool shawl. The celebrations were to be of great importance, and it was nobody's fault that the big day was during my husband's heaviest teaching load. There was no doubt that the family must be complete for the party; and now, with our new airplane, we could get there in four hours, as we had demonstrated. Anyone can arrange four hours to fly, even if one is busy with students, so went the family argument. So, knowing that the significance of birthdays increases with the passing years, we made our plans to be present.

The day before we planned to leave, the weather map in the newspaper was complicated by large rain areas. However, changes are rapid on the Eastern seaboard, and it is useless to telephone the flight forecaster until almost time to start. So I collected my charts and laid them on the floor, and marked in heavy red pencil the course we would follow, and selected my check-points. Then I folded the charts, and laid them in the order in which I would use them. I completed the last detail of the shawl, pressed it, and packed it in a gay box with many flowing ribbons. Very fine and impressive, it looked.

The next morning Frederick had a long discussion with the Weather Bureau. An area of low pressure, the flight forecaster told him, was moving up the coast; but it should not trouble us, for if we started within an hour or two we would get ahead of it. The ceilings were high, but the visibility over the cities was poor: four miles at Philadelphia. It was not expected to get worse during the day. Tomorrow would be worse, he said, and he suggested that we would find better conditions inland. So we decided to go, and I took out the maps and plotted a new course, to avoid the coast and the big cities, and fly instead over the Virginia and Pennsylvania countryside. It would be eight minutes longer, but safer. There are fewer airplanes in the sky there than close around the big airports, and the smoke and haze are likely to be less dense.

So, with charts, shawl box, suitcases and all, we took off. The sky was overcast but the ceiling high, and the visibility not too bad; at three thousand feet we leveled off, on course. As we flew, we composed a verse in praise of grandmas; it was not a good verse, but it could be kept in reserve for use at the dinner, if necessary. High over the tiny community of Jennings Ordinary, Virginia, I wrote down a couplet, checked my navigation for wind drift, and thought of the public house which must once have stood there at the crossroads beneath us, and of how it must have been in the olden days. Of the cider in mugs and the firelight dancing on the bearded faces of the farmers, and the sweating horses bringing riders with news of war, the battles of Manassas and Bull Run. And of Grandma, who was a child then, and her father a Confederate officer, and the many changes she had seen during her long life.

Presently we landed for gas and sandwiches. We were more than halfway there already, but the east wind had blown the smoke from the big cities toward the mountains, and the visibility was getting very poor. But the sky, faint and pale above the smoke, was blue. I knew, from our previous trip, some of the landmarks of the lovely Pennsylvania country over which we flew. Great rich fields and small shiny towns threaded on railroads, like beads on a wire. And I knew that as we approached New York, the towns would increase in size and number until they squeezed out the fields completely, and one town merged into the next. The terrain would become a vast expanse of houses, the suburban area north and west of the city, where an emergency landing was something one didn't dare think of.

Today, in the smoke and haze, the rivers would make the best check-points. We would cross four of them. As always, I glanced at my watch as we left the ground, and then I calculated river times. First, I figured Susquehanna time, twenty-two minutes from now; that will make it three minutes past three, when we should be directly over the great slow-moving water, with a cliff on the east bank, and a power plant and a bridge. Then in seventeen minutes, Schuylkill time, and we should see a winding, twisting stream, looking dirty even before it reaches the outskirts of Philadelphia. And next would be the majestic Delaware, coming through its private Gap in the mountain range, although we wouldn't see that today, I thought sadly. And finally the Hudson, with the George Washington Bridge to tell us our exact position, and then I would feel the surge of delight that always comes to me at the end of a trip, when the vivid sensations of all that I love and hate about flying crowd themselves into my mind, and another bunch of charts are put away in their pocket, and another navigation job has been done. And, a minute or two later, the Croton Dam and the landing at Westchester County.

The air was thickening and the sky was no longer blue. We can't go far wrong, I thought, for we must cross the Hudson somewhere if we hold our compass course, somewhere between the city and Bear Mountain Bridge. So we can certainly find our way, for we have plenty of fuel. Ahead, I saw a bank of heavy cloud, and felt the wheel move forward and the wings tilt down as we lost altitude to pass under it. Such local cloud formations often hang around near rivers, I remembered, and there, ahead, I caught the first glimpse of the water, the Susquehanna, and then we were across it, flying low. Then, close under the wing strut I saw an airport, one which I had not expected; how nice and comforting it looked. But where were we? We circled it. "Do we land?" The affirmative was already on my tongue, when I saw light sky to the east. Together we pointed to it, and as if drawn to an open door, we left the airport and flew on. At Schuylkill time it was darker again and I couldn't find any landmarks. The ceiling was lower, and we went down to keep under it. We flew in thick soup now, following the compass over the Delaware. Not far to the Hudson, if only the clouds will stay up. Go straight on and we'll come to something, there are many airports around here. Straight on, and watch where we go! Plenty of gas, and the engine beat is smooth. We can always turn back and go down the river to Trenton. No need to

worry . . . and yet . . . that town down there . . . I
don't recognize it; and that big double-track railroad?
It must be that one, there on the chart, now I have it.
We followed it until it turned . . . the wrong way . . .
round a hill! *Where* were we? The soup was thicker,
so follow the railroad, down under a cloud mass and up,
only seven hundred feet over a ridge of hills, and there,
big and beautiful in the valley, was a hard-surfaced airport, with three runways in an inviting triangle. No hesitation this time, and down we went into Morristown, and
solid ground and weather news and gas. Marginal
weather was spreading over a large area, they told us,
and we consulted. If Westchester closed in, could we ever
grope our way back here? No, stay here. I had had
enough of the soup. So we tied the Stinson and took a
taxi into town, and watched, fascinated, the Seeing Eye
dogs and their human charges, working the traffic, learning together and teaching each other. But we woke next
morning, Grandma's birthday, to a steady, drenching rain,
and there was nothing we could do except go to the airport, see that the Stinson was safe, rescue the beribboned
package, and take the train for New York. Ten minutes
by air, it was one hour and thirty minutes of a dreary,
shaking train, lurching through a grubby mess of back
yards and laundry, Trees of Heaven and bad smells; and
the package, ribbons damp now, lay on the seat beside me.
Grandma greeted us, from the middle of a pile of tele-
grams, letters and parcels. In the evening we toasted her
in champagne, thinking of the Stinson in the rain at
Morristown.

The next day, the weather was clear. We considered
the prospect of the train with much distaste, and decided
to hire an Aeronca at Westchester County, and fly to
Morristown for the Stinson. I could pilot the small plane,
with Frederick behind me, and he would fly the Stinson
back. I would follow him. The local instructor led us out
to the tie-down line, where I looked suspiciously over
the plane he offered us. He looked, equally with suspicion,
at me. "Check you out," was all he said. (This is a
customary, and very wise, precaution, before a flight
school will rent a plane to an unknown pilot. An instructor flies around the field with you to be sure that
you know how to handle it, and he checks your license
and medical certificate as well.) So, silently, I flew the
pattern with an instructor behind me, and presently he
got out and Frederick got in. As I took off in the little
trainer and headed for Morristown, I was tense. Frederick was behind me, and he knew so much more than I
did, and he had so many more hours and was so much
better a pilot than I was. I wanted with all my heart
to do well, to show myself capable of handling the thing.
Relax! There were those lovely Morristown runways, not
quite so urgently attractive as they had been, just forty-
eight hours ago. Oh, forget him there behind you and do
a decent landing! Down, flare out over the concrete . . .
run along, fine, that was a nice one, and as I pressed on
the brakes the nose started to turn. In spite of all I could
do, we swung around in a horrible, disgraceful ground
loop. At last we stopped turning; the wings, miraculously,
were undamaged, but as I taxied to the hangar ramp I

was red-faced and embarrassed, certain that every pilot in Morristown was there to watch me! We untied the Stinson, and arranged to meet back at Westchester, and Frederick took off and was soon out of sight. And then the Aeronca refused to start. Squat and unco-operative, the wretched thing sat on the pavement shamming dead, while the attendant and his friends worked on it in turn. At last, exasperated, I turned my back on it and walked away, and it started! Were my troubles over? I had had enough for one day. I flew over the houses and the Hudson, and felt better. The control tower cleared me to land on the turf, but my luck was out. I misjudged my height above the grass blades, and I flew wheels first into the ground and bounced. I gave it a burst of power and nosed down, only to hit and bounce again, up and down, all along the grass strip. When it was over, and the Aeronca was tied down and paid for, I walked out of the office to Frederick waiting in the car. He looked surprised.

"Hello," he said, "I didn't see you come in. I was watching a bunch of students doing some awful landings."

"Oh," I replied, "you must have missed me. How very odd!"

And when we got back to the house, there was Grandma. "Why," she said, somehow indignant and waving her stick, "why were you not at my birthday party?"

CHAPTER 5

M_y first flight, my lessons and first solo, and the coming of the Stinson—in fact all the events of my early flying, took place at a tiny airport which was directly north of the town. "Airways," we called it. I think it had been built only a few years; it was one of the neatest airports I have ever seen, and without doubt the smallest. It was always well groomed; the grass was kept mown, and someone (I never knew who it was) kept the weeds from trespassing onto the edges of the stone steps that led up from the parking place. And there were no heaps of junk, broken wings and empty oil drums, the sort usually found at airports, piled not quite out of sight behind the hangar. It was a postage-stamp airport—clean and tidy.

The two runways crossed each other at an acute angle, forming an X with two long and two short arms. The wind sock was on the roof of the big hangar, and there was an office where students kept their logbooks, and an oblong window through which one could watch the airplanes. The runways were very narrow, not wide enough to allow two planes to pass, and at the edges were areas of rough ground, weeds and deep patches of briar. The long runway (as we called it) was all of fifteen hundred feet, and the other was only eleven hundred, so we were taught to use every available foot of space. We must start the take-off run at the extreme end of the strip, and land as close as possible, never more than a third of the way along. The northeast take-off was over bunches of wires which were strung along the main highway, and across the north-south runway there was a cart track; sometimes a mule, pulling a load of tobacco, would move leisurely out of the trees just as a plane approached to land, and the plane would have to go round. As it roared over the driver's head he would look up from under his sunhat of ragged straw, his face a vivid contrast of dark skin and white eyeballs. To the south, the runway had been built up to end above a small hollow, and the wind flowed over the edge with the force of a waterfall. On days after the passage of a cold front, the strong north wind would catch a plane as it came to land, and thrust it down and into the hollow. Unexpectedly, the pilot might find himself level with the strip, even below it, and going down! He would open the throttle wide and the plane would scramble up against the current until it reached the runway, where it would sit down with almost no landing roll, a little breathless after such a struggle.

It was the sort of airport that keeps a pilot busy. There, every landing must be a precise one, and broken wings or smashed gear was the penalty of a ground loop, that horrible uncontrollable spiral that can start out of a swerve on the landing roll. The perfectionists among us enjoyed the necessary attention to detail, and we strove to make every approach as good as possible. We were satisfied to know that, if we could land there, we could sit down anywhere, at any airport, safely. Many times I have stood and watched, I freely admit with a certain mild feeling of superiority, the pilots of visiting aircraft who, used to longer runways, would fly around to look things over. Sometimes they would make the approach many times before they were just right, and slow enough, to manage a landing. And I saw some who never did make up their minds to land! I have often been glad that I learned at a small field, for I learned something I shall never forget.

Among every group of pilots, though, there are the careless, the irresponsible and the inept, and it was these who caused the final closing of the airport that I loved so well. A house has been built on the clay bank of the

strip from which I soloed, and the hollow at the south
end is now a pond. The hangar is gone, and nothing but
memories remain.

At the height of its activity, in the first years after
the war, the airport had, as well as the half-dozen privately owned aircraft which were based there, two tandem
Aeroncas, a Cessna 140 and a Piper Cruiser. They were
for teaching or for rent and were flown by anyone who
had a license, and who could check out in one of them.
Usually those pilots flew at irregular intervals, and were
not quite familiar with the weather conditions, or the
peculiarities of the plane they rented. Often, a crack-up
was the fate of a rented plane. Insurance against damage
to such fragile craft is prohibitive, so that for most airport operators a run of bad luck, with one or two accidents, can be enough to bring financial disaster. It was this
way with Airways, and it happened all at once.

The first to go was the Aeronca Chief, which the
airport took when we bought the Stinson. Within three
weeks, a young man hired it and buzzed his home. He
tangled with the roadside wires and crashed into a small
field, and he walked away with a broken rib. The Chief?
They piled the bits onto a truck and brought it back, with
earth and stones plugging its nose, a poor, ruined, sad
thing—our Chief in which we had had so much fun. He
said that the engine had quit and he had tried to make a
forced landing. But there was a fine big pasture on the
other side of the road, and the wind, as he crashed, was
from behind him.

And then someone rented the Piper and got lost in

the mountains, and was running low in gas. He planned a landing; and, it is said, pulled out the control that leans the mixture, instead of the carbureter heat. So the engine quit and he crashed. Old, familiar, sickening tales!

It was only a Sunday or two later that, at the end of a long and delightful day, we flew the Stinson home from a trip to the seashore. Every plane at the field had been out that day, in perfect weather, and now they were coming home at dusk, like birds to roost. A Taylorcraft landed. I loved to watch them as they touched down, so we joined a small group of pilots, and we stood talking, relaxed and happy. Another came, and now only the old Aeronca, my favorite, was not yet home. The sun was low; surely, I thought, it will be back soon, it has no lights. And then I heard it. Frederick moved toward the car, and, satisfied, I followed him, and I saw the plane, in the darkening sky, lining up with the north runway. I sighed with contentment on the way home.

Next day, as I drove along the road to fly, I saw a truck coming toward me. My heart sank as it passed, for high on it, without wings or propeller, was the fuselage of an Aeronca. It was unmistakable. Something awful must have happened! Thoughts crowded as I drove on; gloomy thoughts. The owner himself was at the airport, and it was worse than I had imagined. He was closing up, then and there; the planes were to be sold. This was the final blow. What had happened? I asked. He had rented the plane to a young man, with only a few hours since his Private license, and the passenger who climbed into the back seat was a huge fellow, who must have weighed over two hundred and fifty pounds. The pilot came in too high and, unused to so much weight in the rear, he stalled, twelve feet above the runway. The plane had crashed down like a stone, and the right wing and landing gear were broken.

In deep distress, I turned my car around and drove home. What would we do now, and where would we go? The Stinson must be moved, and based at some other airport. How could I fly without George, to whom I still turned so often for advice? And that much-loved slowpoke the Aeronca Champion, so perfectly suited for an evening stroll over the fields and woods . . . would I ever fly one again? How could people be so careless, so unappreciative of the lovely things? Why, oh! why? I poured out my miseries to Frederick, and it was then that, at the end of an era, a new one began. Within a few days, we took the Stinson to the huge grass field at Chapel Hill, where we still keep it. And we talked with George, who had done so much for us both, and with the owner of the closed Airways. Once again the incredible happened, and we bought the damaged Aeronca, sharing it with George. I could fly it, and he could use it for teaching. Soon, it was repaired and in good order; and our association lasted for several years until George's plans changed, and the plane became entirely mine. Our teen-aged daughter sniffed when she heard the news. She much prefers sports cars.

"Are you going to get a whole hangar full?" she

said. *"That* old airplane! Will 'e fly?" So we laughed. "Willie Fly" we called him, and Little Willie Fly the Aeronca, he became.

"Why on earth," asked an ignorant acquaintance, "do you want *two* airplanes? Do you each fly one of them when you go the beach?" But the pilots at the airport ask me a question for which I have no answer. "Which do you prefer?" they say.

These are some of the differences. In the Stinson we sit side by side in the roomy front seat, and we can go cross country, comfortably and steadily, at over two miles a minute. The Stinson is heavy and rides well in rough air, flattening the bumps as it flies. It is powerful, and has three times the horsepower of the Aeronca; it is too "hot" an airplane for a student. But if I do not want to go anywhere; if I want only to be alone in the sky for an hour, Little Willie is my choice. In flying it, the stick is held in the right hand, and the left hand operates the throttle. The cockpit is narrow, and the tandem seating allows a symmetrical view from either window, which helps in the accurate judgments to be made in flying maneuvers. The Aeronca has no radio, no lights, and none of the gyroscopic instruments used for flight in clouds. The equipment is of the simplest. The instruments are arranged on the panel differently from those in the Stinson, with its wheel and centrally operated throttle. Yet (perhaps because) the planes are so dissimilar, I can fly either one, or change from one to the other, with never a moment of hesitation. And, unlike the Stinson, the Aeronca is constructed for mild acrobatics; with care to avoid excessive strain in dives and pull-outs, the wings will stay on!

As well as these things, there are the more subtle differences, hard to describe. Among them are some of the sensations that contribute to the delight of flying; the quality of the touch of the controls, of balance, and the smooth pressures of the perfectly co-ordinated turn, the pressures felt so surely on "the seat of one's pants." Maneuvers in the Aeronca are always imperfect. It points up the pilot's mistakes and emphasizes his deficiencies. He must work for what he gets. The Stinson, in contrast, with its inherent stability, seems to help the pilot, and makes him fly better than he expects to. After a few weeks' interval, it is with the Aeronca that I find myself out of practice, a little less accurate in the turns, a little rough on the controls. Then I want to improve again.

Each plane is an individual, different even from its twin. I would know our Stinson among a crowd of Stinsons; our Aeronca among a hundred others. In Willie, as a stall approaches, I hear a warning note in a slight vibration of the plastic windshield; the Stinson sings a song in the tail assembly as it leaves the ground, and whistles gaily as it lands.

Sometimes my satisfaction is in one, sometimes in the other. How can I possibly say which I prefer?

In the years before I flew, I thought of myself as a person prone to sea sickness. A day spent in a small fishing boat on Lake Erie, or a week on a transatlantic leviathan, it made no difference, for I was miserable before I left the dock, all the time during the voyage, and for hours after I landed. In spite of this, I have never been uncomfortable in the air, and to my delight, I found that I enjoyed stalls and spins, and the roller-coaster sensations of acrobatic flight. And now my chance had come for some more advanced air work. I had often thought of loops, which are simple, and yet the most spectacular of the elementary maneuvers, and I wondered whether I could do them. I could, anyway, ask George about them, and one day I did. George told me, first, dive to gain speed. Then pull the stick back steadily and at the same time give it full open throttle. The nose rises and goes on rising, and you are upside down; the earth is above you. Then close the throttle. Relax the back pressure on the stick until you are level once more and that is all. The main danger, as with spins, lies in indecision, in lack of authority. It is essential to get up enough speed in the dive, or the airplane will not rise and turn over, but will stall in a vertical position, halfway up, and begin to fall backwards, out of control. This is the dreaded whip-stall. When the stick is fully back, and the weight of the airplane is on the tail, the elevators can be torn off. With sufficient speed, loops are easy. And at the top of a loop, the gasoline stays in the tank, and the red cap stays on the instructor's head. The pilot does not hang from his seatbelt, nor do his feet come loose from the rudder pedals. A watch on a chain, suspended from the instrument panel, would point, at that moment, straight upward! The test of a good loop, George warned me, is the momentary turbulence as you level off, into air disturbed by your initial dive and pull-up, proof that you have flown a complete circle.

So, next time out, I was shown how to wear a parachute, and how to pull the ripcord. I struggled into the clumsy thing, and we walked to the plane, checked it and climbed in.

"We wear these things," said George, "because regulations demand it. There is no extra strain on the wings if you loop correctly. But, of course, if you *do* have to jump . . ."

The plane climbed high, and for an hour we looped and snap-rolled and spun, while I tried to accept the green fields hanging over my head, and the blue sky at my feet, and the whirling horizon. From behind me, came George's voice. "Good flying is planning and relaxation. Line up with the sun, or with the road. Level your wings. Get up a little more speed before you start back on the stick. Now back, back more, fully back. Get that stick all the way back! Close the throttle as the nose cuts the horizon. . . . Now do another. . . . O.K. You may practice them solo now."

I hardly knew why I went out to the airport the next fine day. Yes, I asked for it, and now it is up to me, I thought. I refused to make plans and a blank settled on my mind. Maybe I could forget. But George understood. "Will you practice loops today?" he asked. He leaned on the wing strut as I fastened my safety belt, and I watched him intently as I listened to his last-minute instructions. Oh, for a sign, any sign, for an excuse, however feeble, to ask him to come with me. But there was only his calm, unspoken assurance that I could do it. "Don't think you are doing anything unusual. Get up enough speed and get the stick back, and you will avoid a whip-stall. Loops are easy. Anything you want to ask?" Oh, yes indeed, George, but I can't ask you!

Once more the formalities of the take-off are completed. The airplane rushes down the runway and up and over the trees, and the solitude and the sweet freedom of the skies are mine. I relax, for there is no hurry, and Willie climbs slowly. But today he climbs most unusually fast, and we are high enough, much too soon. I level off, and my hands are wet and my mouth is dry. I circle the airport, twice. This won't do; it only makes matters worse. Shall I run away? Fly away, anywhere, and never come back? No! Go back down and tell George I couldn't do it? Oh, no! Tighten the safety belt again and face the sun. Dive. Slowly the air-speed indicator moves up, to a hundred, a hundred and ten, a hundred and fifteen miles an hour. Then pull back on the stick, slowly at first as the nose comes up. Then faster back, up and back some more, hard back until the stick is tight against your belly, and your arm is hooked around it to keep it there. The nose is straight up. Look, for an everlasting moment the blue sky is at your feet, and you are rising, drawn up, forever up and away. Smoothly the plane turns over and the horizon comes tumbling from behind, hurrying over your head. Cut the gun! Then, when you face the fields, let go the stick, slowly and steadily. The plane bumps and shivers as it passes through its own propeller wash, making a complete circle. It is in straight and level flight, facing the sun.

That day I looped and looped some more, and went home contented.

For a while, it was hard to get used to the idea that Airways was gone, and that the big Airport-on-the-Hill was now our home. The unbelievable luxury of the huge expanse of grass; three instead of two runways to choose from. They were almost wide enough, I figured, to take off crosswise; and each one was about a mile long. It was almost too easy. I swore to myself that I would not become lazy and forget the rigorous discipline of my early days. The hangar was well built, of concrete and metal, and there was a concrete apron, with some tie-down ropes.

At first, I flew the pattern. I learned the peculiarities of the terrain of each approach, and of each take-off. Using the standard left-hand pattern, I found a small hill at the northwest end, with a wooded hollow. Watch, I decided, for down drafts, there, and keep enough altitude to get around the hill. Another runway ended in a wide road and a field, where up drafts were likely. And I noted the places which might be useful in case of an engine failure on the take-off, and the areas which were dense with houses, to be avoided at any cost.

Very soon, we began to talk to the other pilots, and sometimes we sat together on a bench, hangar-flying, laughing and teasing each other. Any argument, I noticed, was settled by an appeal to an elderly, vigorous man—

"Poppa," they called him—an instructor who had taught flying for many years. He sat in the sun holding court, surrounded by his students, talking sometimes of his experiences, but more often of airplanes and their habits, of what was safe practice and what was not, and of flight in fact and in folklore. There seemed to be no end to his knowledge of aircraft, of their strengths and their weaknesses, and their diseases and how to cure them. Often a student who had recently soloed would fly the pattern in Poppa's Cub, while we sat there and the instructor, with his expert eye, noted and commented. I thought: I know just what it feels like to land in front of a critical audience. I was glad that my first few landings were good ones, and I was glad, in some ways, that I had grown up and graduated. It was time for me to go out into the world, and to make my own decisions as to wind and weather, decisions to fly or not to fly. I needed the responsibility, I knew, to give me self-confidence. But there was so much still to be learned, that it was fine for me to have Poppa there, and I soon developed a great respect for his experience, the width of his knowledge and his irreproachable technique.

One afternoon, my friend Peggy and I arranged to meet at the Airport-on-the-Hill. Peggy is younger than I am, with a family of four, still in school. A colored butler drives her children back and forth over the several miles from the white-pillared house to the town. In Peggy's leisurely routine, telephone calls are unwelcome before the morning is half over. She has calm blue eyes and grey streaks in once black hair, which is carefully waved around her head; her movements are smooth. What an excellent pilot she would be, I thought one evening after dinner, when the talk had turned to flying. She had seemed astonished, and really envious, that there should be people living in her community who did such strange things and had such fun. But at the suggestion that she should come and try it herself, I caught the glance toward her husband, and the straightened mouth line, at the thought of the emptiness of the sky. But then I saw a spark in her eye, and her husband nodded. It would be fun to give her the chance, I thought. Who knows? She might get the disease herself. So I telephoned her, and, as I half expected, she had a headache.

"Oh," she said, "I'm so sorry, and please do call me again." I knew the signs; it was hard for her, and it took her many days to make up her mind, but this day at last there was no headache, and she was at the airport, and it was too late to turn back.

But since my telephone call some clouds had grown up, some of them thick and dark. We stood, Peggy and I, on the steps watching them, to see how fast they moved and where, and I looked for cumulus cauliflowers with lightning in them, and listened for the sound of distant thunder. There were none of these things, and the wind was calm, so we pulled the Aeronca out from the hangar. Poppa came, and together we checked it, and again we watched the sky.

"There's no wind in that," said Poppa, pointing to a

cloud, "and it'll move up Danford way, up the river. But watch to the west, in case of a storm. You can always get in ahead of it, if one should come up."

We took off. The clouds seemed, from the air, to be harmless enough, with clear space between them in plenty, and under them, too. The sky looked strange, though, with patches of haze spread around, mostly in the cloud shadows, not just the usual faint sort that softens the horizon. A sort of haze which might well be nothing but the effect of alternating light and shade, a diffuse sunbeam, and yet it might be more than that . . . it seemed a little unusual. I flew, keeping well out in the clear, in pleasant sunshine, and we circled Peggy's house, waving to the children who danced on the lawn. Presently we came back to the airport. One of the clouds had settled over the village, but there was room enough, and in fact I felt sure one could land easily, under it. I approached from the north, relaxed and casual, as I lost altitude to make my usual pattern for landing. Then, as a canoe is caught in a current and swept into swirling rapids, my airplane pitched and twisted as I worked at the stick and rudders. Caught and held in the turmoil, back and forth and up and down, we were thrown, out of control, lurching in the sky. Turn back, I told myself, where you came from, and push forward on the stick to gain some speed. And then we were in still air once more. We had stepped, unaware, from a firm river bank into a raging torrent, and had scrambled out again; but the edge of the bank . . . where was it? Such turbulence, from so ordinary a cloud, needed some consideration, so we flew around before I tried again. Then, using an old trick, I came toward it at a tangent, feeling for the edge of the bank, like a blind man with a cane, my hands alert on the throttle and controls. And we were in it again; it hit us a slanting blow, and we turned away. We had fallen a second time into the invisible rushing river, but this time I was ready, and at once we reached solid air again. I saw the runways, almost below us, and the strange cloud. Could we manipulate the rapids and land safely? How low down did the turbulence reach? Right to the ground? I strained my eyes to see the wind sock, but we were too far away. We could, of course, go to another airport; we had enough gas, and plenty of time before dark, but our cars were down there, and perhaps there were other clouds, worse ones, elsewhere. And Peggy, how was she feeling?

Hesitating, I flew on, and I was lonely now. I looked for other planes, and there were none. Alone in the sky, lonely, with a helpless companion. She touched my shoulder and I looked around.

"Bumpy there, wasn't it?" I smiled back at her. Loneliness is in the sky, but presses never so fiercely upon you as when you are with a helpless friend. Still undecided, I wandered, and then I saw in the distance a tiny plane come from behind the cloud, like a little black insect, low down, heading for the field. As it came near I recognized it. My confidence came surging back, for it was Poppa's Cub, and he, I was sure, was flying it. I had company, and I had faith in him, and I would follow him, for he would do the safe thing. I was all right, in fact I was fine. He was up in that mess and planning to land, and so, too, could I. I saw him start a straight-in approach, very fast. Very fast, indeed, he came over the edge of the runway, and instead of slowing as I expected, he tore along, barely skimming over the grass, past the hangar and on, out over the woods. For God's sake, I thought, he's landing down wind! Round the field went the Cub, and in again for another try, at full speed, entirely too fast. I crept nearer, very carefully, to see the wind sock, but I found no rough air, and I saw the sock, standing out, straight and stiff, in a very strong wind. And there he was, coming in with it, instead of against it. This made no sense, none at all. The first lesson a student learns, the first day he touches the controls, is to face the wind, to use it to lift you as you take off, and to brake you as you land. Evidently he had gone mad; there was no other way of explaining his behavior. But I was still all right. The wind was strong, yes, but steady. Low down, it was not like the rapids under the cloud, and one can meet an enemy who attacks from the front. I would be independent and land my own way, and look after myself and forget his antics. I got down lower, and in order to face exactly into the gale, I headed the plane crosswise over the corner where the two runways meet. There would be no trouble stopping when I was on the ground, not on a day like this. I saw the Cub, far away, so I came down some more, fast and low over the treetops, forgetful of my passenger, concentrating on getting down, down into the teeth of the wind. A moment of delight, the delight of battle! Level your wings! We touched, and with the stick held forward and the tail up we ran along the turf as if we were glued to it. A moment later the tail dropped, and we were safe under the lee of the hangar. And there in the door stood Poppa, fidgeting and biting his nails, furious at the student up there in his plane. We could see it now, circling low, just as I had done, and as we watched it came, just as I had done, sideways across the trees and safely, this time, into the wind.

As we put our plane away and closed the hangar doors, the Cub's engine stopped and a boy got slowly out. Silently and elaborately, the two of them, instructor and student, tied the plane to its ropes and chocked the wheels. Politely but firmly, the instructor said good night to us, and we moved away. I never knew what was said, but there was nothing I could do anyway. I have not seen the student again, but Peggy has flown with me, many times.

The long spell of fine weather broke, and it was winter. The heavy rain cleared only to freeze, and snow followed. The thick red clay of the airfield, soaking wet, heaves up when the frost gets into it. And then, after the thaw, it is deceptively smooth and fine, and very soft; ready, like leavened bread, to collapse at a touch. Airplanes are trapped as they taxi, and must be pulled out of the mess.

The snow lay six inches deep on the land, to melt at last in the sun. Out at the airport, after two weeks of being grounded, I expected only to look at the airplanes, but I found that the snow had flattened the clay surface as if with a huge roller, and the ground, though wet, was hard. To get a take-off run into the wind, and over the highest part of the field, I pulled Willie the Aeronca up against the bank, where I warmed up and checked the magnetos. Then very slowly I opened the throttle, and slowly, very slowly, we began to move. Spray rose around us as we gathered speed. Suddenly, Willie flew, with a little jump into the air. Like a seal that slips from a rock into the ocean, so the air folded close around the wings, and the controls became firm. We gained security as we nosed upward.

Two weeks without flying, a long time for me. I checked the landmarks carefully, half expecting that the snow blanket might have flattened them, too. I climbed to two thousand feet and turned southwest, and flew, happily, into the wind until I reached the river where it crowds around under a bluff. There is a village on the bluff, and upstream there are rapids, usually very shallow and full of boulders. Today, as I expected, the river was in spate, and I circled down to look. Down and down, until I could see the pattern of the flood current as it slid round the boles of the trees. From the turmoil which hid the boulders, great crests of pale foam were pushed out, and they turned and hesitated a moment before they rushed away. The river was a racing, whirling flood. Lower I went, past a large black bird flapping slowly out of a tree. Desolate expanses of muddy yellow, with dark shadows and pale blotches of foam, the colors of the water were matched by those of the trees and fields. Bare sycamore trees lined up where the river bank should be, their huge yellow trunks inlaid with ivory, and in the fields the yellow ochre of the sedge grass was edged with the snow, which still lay in the shady places. And the bird was black, and glittered in the sun.

I flew upstream, very low, along the main channel, following closely the bends in the river. There were many islands, flood-made, I supposed. Few houses, and no people. What lives in that wild water? Up miles and miles of flooded river I flew, over quiet deep places and flooded meadows, and past a bridge, one span of which had collapsed, leaving the pillar standing alone in the water, still holding on to a mass of twisted metal. Then I came to the big dam, where the water poured over the spillway, and I could hear it, even against the engine noise, thundering onto the rocks. I turned and headed for home.

Presently I was in the pattern, and I could see the water in shining puddles on the runways. The horizon dipped behind the trees and I was almost down, when my fingers pushed forward on the throttle, the engine roared, and I went up again. Why should I land, when I didn't want to? This time I headed for the power station to the north, where the two tall chimneys stand. A mile or so upstream from it is our favorite picnic place, a sandy cove surrounded by woods of beech and mountain laurel. There are huge grey rocks, a ruined mill overgrown with ferns, and the broken millrace. Of the roads to the mill, along which so many horses must have dragged their heavy loads of grain, there are now only a few traces here and there, a low wall of loose stone, hard to follow among the trees. I have walked there often, and flown over it, too, but today it was different. From my place, circling a few hundred feet up, I could see into the long-forgotten past. For a few hours only, the old roads had come to life again, for they lay outlined, clear and double, by the snow which still remained in the tracks. They were unmistakable; white lines on the dark earth, three roads converging on the mill, crossing and recrossing the little rivulet in the valley and then spreading fanwise, to join the old highway, which was deserted when the new motor road was built. And near the highway I could see, in woods which had once been fields, traces of the furrows which had been ploughed back and forth across them, many years ago.

The blond boy in the black and silver plane went down into the woods.

Three days had passed since a cold front and the sky was china blue and the wind warm and very gentle. What a day to fly! I went out in the early afternoon, to work on maneuvers. From the hangar ramp where I stood, I saw the black one, the single seater NX (experimental category) plane rise up over the hills to the west, from the small field where it was based. It landed, and was filled with gas; we talked and laughed for the pleasure of the lovely day and the airplanes. I knew and liked the blond boy; last year he flew a lot from Airways, where he had kept a Luscombe in the hangar, but we all backed away and became very busy when he offered us rides. Many times I had seen him take off alone, climbing and spinning, tumbling and looping, like a crazy thing. Now he spoke of his delight in the power of the NX, and how he had brought it from Texas three weeks ago. He took off just ahead of me, with a rush. He held it a yard off the sod for a mile of runway, and then he hung it straight up on the propeller, and disappeared into the blue. What a show-off! But we all, I think, envied him such a thing to play with. I flew, too, in the little old Aeronca, feeling very sedate and slow, up to three thousand feet, spins to the right and left, a few stalls and turns and back home. I fetched my tools and sat on the grass to adjust the bolt on the steerable tail wheel. Presently Poppa and two other pilots came and watched me, and began the usual teasing that I endure whenever my hands get dirty. We talked of the characteristics of the NX plane, and of the blond boy.

"A natural. A daredevil at first, but he's grown out of that. He can look after himself."

We sat, contented, on the steps in the peace and the sunshine. A car drove up, and a man got out, striding urgently toward us.

"There's a plane cracked up a mile down the road. Black and silver. The man in it is dead." The peace and the pleasure shrank up and left me shivering in the hard light. The weather-beaten faces around me barely changed, as with competent and deliberate pace the three men set about doing what had to be done. The instructor took charge.

"You go and see that no one touches the wreck, or lights a match near it. . . . You telephone the Aviation Safety Office, and file the accident report. . . . I know his wife; I suppose I must tell her. His car is at the small field. I wonder where he left the keys."

I asked the man, had he seen this thing happen? He had been hunting in the woods, and had heard the plane, motor running hard, just before it hit the road, nose down in a dive, and bounced against a tree. He ran to it. The blond boy in the cockpit gasped and died, all broken up. The black plane, broken, too.

A half hour ago and a mile away, the blond boy was having fun in the lovely sky. Then came the last seconds, the panic, the struggle, and the rending, tearing crash. So unbelievable and yet so to be believed, an end, a finality.

Minutes later, the crowds, the newsmen, the photographers came. They covered the cockpit with torn wing fabric and did their work. Then came the Aviation Safety people, to investigate. Why had he, an accomplished pilot, been unable to level out, slow his speed and land in a stall, the way we all are taught to do in a crisis? Why did he lose control? Did he black out? Did the controls freeze or break? Did he spin too low, without altitude to recover, and hit in the ensuing dive? No one will ever know.

"You're kidding me," his wife said. "What? You mean he will never come back to me, ever again?"

CHAPTER 6

During the night a front passed over the Piedmont Plateau, and by the time we woke it was already out to sea. It was in mid-September. We took off in high spirits into a sparkling, well-washed sky, to fly north along the east slope of the Appalachian mountain range. We hoped to travel almost the entire length, over more than a thousand miles of venerable mountains. Among the most ancient in the world, their profiles are now worn smooth and rounded, but they still show the pattern of their formation, the regular parallel ridges, oriented northeast to southwest. Upheavals of long ago must have squeezed the earth's surface, as the fingers of a gigantic hand might squeeze a pastry crust rolled out flat. In Virginia and North Carolina the rivers, which rise in the mountains and eventually flow southeast across the plain to the sea, run at first northeast in the valleys between the ridges before they turn, every one of them at a right angle as they emerge into the plain. Another upheaval must have changed the levels of the valley floors, and altered the river courses, and bent them so. Now they flow *uphill,* I found myself thinking. Uphill? Why is north up? After all those years of navigating, too!

For the first few hours, the land was familiar. Our course was forty degrees. We had flown this way before. We went along the Blue Ridge, over the Virginia farms with their big cattle sheds and barns, and grazing fields for horses. Then our way would be over the Potomac and into the rolling Pennsylvania hills, and past the Poconos and Catskills (this would be new for us). Up the Hudson valley to Burlington, with the Adirondacks to the west and the Green Mountains to the east. Then (we hoped: this seemed very far away) across the northern tip of Lake Champlain and out into the flat glacial valley of the St. Lawrence, perhaps even to Montreal before dark.

It was a rare day. The Blue Ridges were perfectly named, blue and crystal clear, wave after wave of them. As we flew along the eastern edge we passed over an occasional outcrop which stood away from the orderly ranks; a solitary hill, or one or two little ones together. The cultivated fields pressed close around them, but the tops of the slopes were covered with trees, looking, from above, like humped beds of thick, comfortable moss. Here and there, the autumn colors began to show, a touch of apricot, or the yellow spike of a tulip tree. From Point-of-Rocks we could see the buildings of Washington, and beyond, where the Potomac widens, the water on the horizon gleamed silvery bright. The airport at Frederick, Md., was directly ahead of us; we crossed the river on course, passed over the many-colored mosaic of the little rectangular ponds of a fish-breeding station (so marked on the chart) and came into the pattern to land.

Presently, gas tanks filled and sandwiches eaten, we went on, bearing slightly more to the east. The cities of Bethlehem and Allentown, usually hidden in a mess of their own smog which drifts for miles with the wind, were clear today. Fine-looking towns, I decided; almost beautiful. After we passed them we deliberately lost some altitude and flew, rather low, through the Delaware Water Gap and along the river. Now the land was new to us. We had not flown this way, nor ever driven on the roads below us. On our left we were surprised to see a huge area of hills and valleys, covered with forest, a hostile, monotonous expanse. Here and there, a thin road would penetrate into it, and disappear. I saw no villages, nor even groups of houses; the roads wandered aimlessly. Below us was the river valley, which is divided from the plain by a narrow line of hills. In contrast to the menacing forest, these were friendly, sunny-looking hills, with little bright blue lakes precariously balanced on the summits, and open spaces with curiously shaped buildings, in clearings in the woods. I would have liked to land there, and walk all day in those hills, but we flew on. Someday I would go back. Beyond the hills, the plain, speckled with towns and villages, spread toward New York, less than sixty miles away.

At Port Jervis we left the Delaware where it turns northwest, and we went straight on until we came out into the Hudson valley at Kingston, where we landed for the second time. Then we crossed the Hudson, flying higher now, and went up the east bank. I could see the peaks of the Catskills, which rose within a few miles to over four thousand feet. The hills of New England were to the right, beautifully clear in the afternoon sun. We passed the factories near Albany, and the busy river and railroad yards of Troy and Mechanicsville. On and on, into vacation country. Along the green water of Lake George, with its speedboats darting like insects, leaving their V-shaped trails behind them. Then along Lake Champlain and the narrows at Port Henry, and the wide central part, with the Adirondacks beyond. The Green Mountains closed in toward the lake shore as we came to Burlington.

On the ground again, we consulted. We had made good time; seven hours and ten minutes flying, and an hour at the two landings. Montreal was forty-five minutes away, and we had an hour yet till sundown. There was not a cloud in the sky. As quickly as possible, we completed the formalities of leaving the country, and

filed a Flight Plan. We took off and flew diagonally over
Lake Champlain where it is divided into two by a long
neck of land, over a road bridge and an island or two,
and we saw the railway bridge and Rouses Point, the
little border town at the head of the lake. Below us was
the main highway, and there, on both sides of the road,
were the big flat sheds and parking areas and gates of
the customs and immigration stations. We were over it;
past it; we were in Canada. The highway pointed the
way. In that last half hour, we flew in a different air,
over strange country. The quiet of the evening sky came
on us as the land flattened, and not a ripple stirred. The
sun was low in the west. There was a new character to
the villages. Now in the center of every one of them, there
was a delicate spire of silver, a steeple which flashed fire
in the rays of the sun. The fields were as level as if they
had been pressed by a huge roller, and in the distance
were two or three isolated, sharply pointed hills, sticking
up out of the plain. Then we saw a bigger hill, Montreal
itself, and the river at the foot of the rocky prominence.
And Dorval airport, a busy place with a sleepy name, was
just across the river. The cars on the road began to shine
their headlights, the city began to twinkle, and as we
circled the airport, I saw the lighted cross, huge and high
in the park on top of Mount Royal.

What does the experience of such a day leave behind
it? A day of the gradual unfolding of impressions, one
after the other, to be gathered up and kept, and brought
out again later, many times. Mountains and plains, and

rivers winding among them. Houses, the huge crowds of them that make the cities, and the tiny groups at the crossroads. Railroads, forests, much more forest than I had ever imagined. We had flown that day over places that were, some of them, familiar to us from the ground. How was it possible, I wondered, to drive on the roads and be so unaware of the shape of the country over which one moves? And of what lies behind the wall, in the next valley, or beyond the hill? All the things we had seen did not, as one might expect, make a bewildering confused mass of detail. They made an integrated, vivid picture of a thousand miles of a great mountain range, with all its varying contours and characters; of a rich and populated plain, and the flat seashore fringed by the big cities. From three thousand feet, we could see the world laid out before us, from Mount Mitchell to the towers of Manhattan, a magnificent country of contrasts, archaic and modern, eternal and fragile.

And as we flew, I thought of the Stinson that carried us in such security. Fifty years ago, no man had been able to see what we had seen; and if, five years ago, someone had suggested that I might travel, and navigate, along the Appalachian mountains in my own airplane, it would have sounded utterly incredible!

We put the Stinson into a hangar at Dorval, and we went into Montreal. I knew already that the flight was unforgettable. We spoke little; we were deeply satisfied.

Three days later we came back to Dorval on a dark, bleak morning. As the taxicab drew up at the entrance to the terminal building, I saw the revolving amber light on the control tower which means Instrument Flight Rules. For us it spelled: wait, the visibility is less than three miles. The man at the weather station expected improvement later, so we hoped to be able to take off. I sat where I could watch a runway, where a few planes were landing, appearing suddenly out of the gloom. I could see a tree in the distance, and then presently another beyond it. Visibility was improving; hadn't they said it would? I ran out to the other side of the building, but the amber light was still burning. Back again, and the trees had vanished! But at last the light went off and the field was open. Just beyond the river the skies cleared, and we reached Burlington again.

From Burlington, it was a short flight over the mountains, past Whiteface (how many times I had climbed it!) to land at Lake Placid, where the family was vacationing. They have not got used to our new sport. They have to endure our (to them) unpredictable arrivals and departures, seasoned with endless talk of charts, fronts, VFR and head winds. They still feel that it is much simpler (and safer) to drive. So when, a few days later, our niece had to be fetched from camp near Laconia, N. H., to Lake Placid, we welcomed the chance to demonstrate the utility of our beautiful Stinson. We could fly the Green Mountains and be back for supper, instead of spending a whole day circumnavigating Lake Champlain in a car. The weather people at Burlington reported an extensive high, with nothing worse than haze. And very hazy it was, as, with my brother in the back, we slid around Whiteface Mountain again and over the lake, into the Connecticut valley and out of the hills to Laconia. But somehow the camp had got our signals crossed, and our niece was not at the airport, and when we finally got together, it was late afternoon. We could, I suppose, have made it in time, but I don't like flying in haze, in mountains and into the setting sun. It is not dangerous, but it spoils the fun. And anyway, what was the hurry? Maybe tomorrow would be clearer. So we tied down, bought toothbrushes in the village, and spent a pleasant night.

Next morning, more of the same, but at any rate the sun was behind us. We made ready for take-off, while waiting for a weather sequence. Niece and baggage packed in the back, we were ready to go. But the navigator stayed in the office, watching the tape. "Oh, why wait," said the pilot. "It's just like yesterday." And then it came. Burlington, Vt., overcast, ceiling seven hundred (it must be seven thousand! Could they have missed a zero?) No, it was seven hundred, and those mountains! I ran to the airplane, and we gathered for a council. We couldn't fly straight, but we could perhaps reach Lebanon and then go south of the mountains and into the flat valley. From Lebanon, after a talk with a helpful weatherman, we reached Rutland without trouble. But the visibility was getting worse, and while we waited, an airliner landed from Montreal, bringing a report of patchy instrument conditions, and Burlington was still less than one thousand. The mess, it appeared, was mainly in the valley. If we could get over the lake and up the west side, or to Burlington and then across, the rest should be easy. So we would try. We flew low, along the railroad, past some quarries and factories, past the old disused branch that goes west and crosses the lake at Ticonderoga. It was there that I first saw them, a few pale, discrete clouds, over to the east where the mountains were hiding, hanging very low and light against a dark background. But only a few, and quite isolated. We flew on along the tracks, straining our eyes for landmarks, until we met a whole row of the things, right across our path, like warning arms outstretched. So we doubled back down the railroad, the tenuous thread which would lead us back to safety. We still hoped, and wanted, so badly, to get home for lunch. The west seemed to get lighter, and paler, low down near the ground. By mutual consent, fools that we were, we turned down the disused line to try and cross the lake . . . and we went, slap, with no warning, into a fog bank.

Very suddenly, nothing but greyness. Altitude one thousand or less. Back on the wheel and up, into momentary light. Turn and dive. A flash of fields in front of us, through the stuff, then gone again. An air-speed-indicator needle creeping up, up to where it shouldn't be! Back, oh! back on the wheel, fast but not fast. Another glimpse of fields, and another, and we were in the clear, straight and level and shaken. Scared sick and silly, the navigator took a firm grip on the controls, and refused to let go. Back to Rutland we went. Safe on the ground, we telephoned the parents to come and get us, and the pilot and the navigator walked out in the gloom to the far end of the longest runway, in strained silence. There, in ten fiery minutes, we made many important decisions. The Stinson was for sale (dirt cheap at that moment). The navigator would not fly again with the pilot, if he could not do better than collide with a fog bank. The pilot objected vigorously (and reasonably) to the navigator grabbing the controls. And various other details, including divorce. That settled, we returned to the others, played endless games of horseshoes, found lobster sandwiches at an eating house (delicious leftovers from a wedding breakfast), stuffed ourselves and sat, bored to tears, counting cars on the highway until, long after dark, the family arrived. They remarked, as we drove home through the mountains in the night, in and out of dense fog patches, on a rough and winding road, that they were not convinced of the essential utility of private aircraft! What a day!

As I look back at that flight, and consider the details of it, I see that we *did* have warning. That light stuff, so near the ground, I'll never push it again. That trip taught us both a lot.

A week later we got a lift back over the bumpy mountain roads, to Rutland and the Stinson. We flew between two high hills, and out into the valley of the Hudson. As we flew south, the air became thicker, and the pleasant white clouds disappeared. I was glad when we reached the river, for we could fly along it, and by that time, in the late afternoon, the visibility was very poor. The altimeter read twenty-five hundred feet. The sky was pale and cloudless, but the sun cast no shadows. The towns, clustered on the riverbank, passed beneath us, but they passed unseen. There was no shape visible from the Stinson, nothing ahead, nothing around us, except that far below I could see the river, flat and shiny, a coppery snake. We were in thick haze.

I, the navigator, planned my strategy, with the chart and ruler on my knee, and one eye, always, on the river. We needed gas at Poughkeepsie. Watch for the three bridges that mark the town, fly on along the river a half inch, that is four miles, exactly two minutes; turn ninety degrees, heading due east . . . then one inch, eight miles, four minutes . . . circle and let down, if I did my job well . . . directly over the airport. The beat of the engine makes a song; half inch, four miles, two minutes . . . one inch, eight miles, four minutes. Watch the glittering, coiling snake! At last I see the bridges, the position indicators I need. People cross the river there, on massive concrete and iron, but to me, those three thin lines are feelers, cat's whiskers. Don't start the timing too soon. Directly over the bridges, now . . . and six minutes later we saw the airport runways and we were down.

The weatherman was pleasant and helpful. We should fly high over the hills at Bear Mountain, and the other side was clear. He was right, too, for though at four thousand feet we never saw the bridge or the gorge, soon Long Island Sound and the city of New York lay spread out beautifully before us. In the evening sunshine the shadows darkened the western edges of the fields, as we flew on across the Sound to land at West Hampton. We slept there.

He is fortunate who, through his knowledge of a skill, can appreciate the details of a fine performance. The tiny drama we saw today was a lovely thing, an exhibition of perfection in judgment and instant decision and technique. There were few witnesses; among them I think I was alone, an onlooker with special privilege, my pilot's ticket in my pocket.

It was a fine day, and Long Island is an attractive place over which to fly. It is well groomed and orderly, and a landing could be made on almost any field, except at the extreme east end, where it is almost deserted. The scrubby seashore growth still has possession there. We flew to the most easterly airport, and landed on a sandy strip, and were met and taken to Montauk Point. We sat on the lawn of a house on the cliff top, a hundred feet above the narrow beach where the Atlantic breakers rolled among the rocks, sending spray to the foot of the cliff. On a hillock near us a wooden Indian, twelve feet of him, stared out to sea, shading his eyes with his hand.

While we lunched on the lawn, several groups of navy fighter planes passed, very low along the shore line. They flew in formation, in twos or threes, barely higher than the cliff, and then they went around the bend and out of sight. The west wind was behind them. Then right in front of us as we watched, an engine coughed and died. Before we knew what had happened, the plane had swung out of formation, in a graceful turn, up and over the house. It came back into the wind, as we ran to the edge of the cliff. We stood there, gasping, as it came low over us, just clear of the roof, and sank down toward the sea. Close over the water, beyond the breakers, it slowed for a full stall landing, flaps down, nose up. For an awful moment it hung there, stalled; then it fell into a hissing fountain of water and steam. We saw the pilot climb out and onto a wing. He reached back into the cockpit, and then stood upright, balancing. Unhurried, he stared into the cockpit again, and after a long pause he turned away. He dived into the sea and swam toward the shore. His two companion airplanes came back and circled, as useless to him as their shadows that passed over the wreck. He waved, and they flew away. The plane, ditched in shallow water, did not sink. The beach below us, deserted until now, became suddenly populated. Swarms of small boys appeared out of nowhere, and some ran into the water to help the swimmer. Ashore, through the breakers, he came, and slowly, as if he were very tired, he walked along the beach to the Coast Guard station, the central figure of a milling crowd.

I watched him intently as he moved, as if by so doing I could drag his feelings from him. I longed to ask him how he felt, and what had happened to him during those moments. I wanted to climb down the cliff and pour out questions, and receive a flood of answers, but I was remote from him and helpless. I was divided from him by the elaborate code rules of human conduct, even more surely than the wreck in the waves was divided from the two who had circled over it. Was he sad for the ruined airplane? Perhaps he loved it, the way I might feel, and the long, slow moment before he dived from it might have been a farewell. Or was he elated at the lovely performance he had made? The decision, the turn into the wind, the textbook water landing at the slowest possible speed, full stall, and the perfect choice of position, in the shallow water. Had he flown it many hours, or was it new and strange to him, tricky and unpredictable as unfamiliar aircraft can be? Had he any indication of what was to happen? I shall never know, but I hope, very much, that the event was vivid to him; that it was not, even though he might thus describe it, "just another forced landing."

The next day we saw the reports of the accident in two New York daily papers. The accounts were recognizable to us only by our identification of the time and place of the event. I clipped them with amusement; one had the plane at three thousand feet "plummeting into the ocean," and the other describes the dramatic rescue of the pilot by a Coast Guard cutter. And the name of the Coast Guard station (believe it or not!) is Ditch Plains!

Our direct route home was over water, too much water, so we flew back over Long Island, and then turned southwest, and across Chesapeake Bay to Richmond. It was disgraceful that, after Richmond, the navigator decided that she preferred to be lazy. Why not make use of US 1, that fat, straight road that we could see so far ahead? It would lead us almost home. Here, the road is to the west of the railroad. There, it dips under as they cross. Now it makes a half circle as it skirts a town, but the railway goes straight through. They cross again, another perfect check-point. The big military airport at Blackstone is off to the west, all alone in the middle of the countryside. Presently the road makes an excursion, but the railroad goes on, toward the two bridges over the Roanoke River. Relaxed and comfortable, we follow the iron compass. Somewhere below, Virginia becomes North Carolina, and we are flying over familiar ground. We leave the road now and fly a course, and soon the ground is spread with well-known landmarks and I watch carefully for the first sight of the Hill. My favorite airport; I like it, more than any other in the world! I catch sight of it, like a great pale starfish on the horizon. Now I perform a small, private ceremony. I carefully fold my charts and put them in the map pocket; then I put on some lipstick, powder my nose and smooth my hair. My job is done. I feel a surge of pleasure at the completion of the trip; at the anticipation of being home again; at the recapturing of the fun we have had; all mixed, deep inside, with regret that one more flight can never be made again. There ahead of us, growing larger and clearer every moment, is the starfish, a funnel which leads from the skies to the earth, a narrow entrance through which we will find our way back to the chores of daily life. Like bees around their hive, several planes are circling. There is no crowding or pushing; each pilot takes his turn, and creeps down the communicating passage, to be swallowed up in the multitudes and go about his business, thinking of when he will return, and get up again into the sky.

Frederick eases back on the throttle to lose altitude.

We could glide home now, if we had to! We join the planes in the pattern. Down until the grass-blades and the wheels touch, and the Stinson bumps over the wiry tufts as we taxi to the gas tanks. We put it into the hangar and transfer our suitcases to the car. We are back home.

We wanted to go to a meeting, to be held in a town some ninety miles away. It was to be an evening affair, and several of our associates were planning to go, by car of course. They would return that night, with less than two hours to drive. But we? We would fly there, *and* back at night if the weather was good. The distance was no more than that of a trip around the countryside on a Sunday afternoon, and an extensive winter high gave us clear, cold air, and perfect visibility was forecast for the area, with a full moon. And we knew how to land the Stinson at night; we had each had about an hour of night-landing instruction. It would be so much faster and easier, too.

We drove our car to the airport; that took fifteen minutes. We opened the hangar and pushed out the Stinson, checked the gas and oil supply and started and warmed the engine. With high heels, my best winter coat and even a hat on my head, I climbed in. We took off in the late afternoon; another fifteen minutes, thirty now. Through the sky, straight and unswerving, we kept our course on an invisible road, and every thirty seconds a mile went by as the highway moved back and forth beneath us, first one side and then the other. I looked at the tiny cars, and wondered which of them contained our poor, earth-bound colleagues. We passed over them so easily and deliciously. In forty minutes we were over the enormous airport of our destination, and we landed and taxied up the interminable concrete to the tie-down area near the control tower. It was not easy to find our way; but guided by the tower's radioed instructions, we went in and out of a maze of taxiways and runways, crossing each other, until we found the grassy field, with chains set in the earth, to which we could tie our airplane. Flight, taxi, tie-down, altogether an hour, and now the grand total stood at one hour and a half. And still we were some eight miles from the town, and exactly on the side away from our destination. So we took a slow and jolty taxi ride, to the town and through it, until we were there. Faster than a car? It depends on your point of view.

At ten thirty, our hosts insisted that they take us to the airport, so after coffee we all drove out. I was conscious, on that night more than usual, of the mixed emotions that our flying engenders in those around us. It sets us apart; remote. We are unique, and more than a little crazy. We are surrounded by a sort of aura, and our world is shared only by others who fly. As we drove to the airport, a night flight in a tiny single-engined plane was before us, and in the eyes of our friends I saw the mingled envy, and admiration, and relief, and a desire to understand why we had chosen to do this, and what it was that drew us up, to wander in the sky. I was conscious, too, of my own feelings, for I was facing something new, and I tried to guess what it would be like, and how the moonlight might affect the check-points of a well-known landscape. How much could we see at night from above? Was I afraid of the trip? I asked myself; and I answered, no, not afraid. I was excited and a little tense; anticipating and half dreading the report of the weatherman, on which our decision to go, or not, would rest. And, as always when I am thinking of airplanes, I was filled with a strange sense of awareness, as if living were concentrated, an hour into a few minutes, and my senses were somehow sharpened and polished.

Together we climbed the winding stair that led to the office of the Weather Bureau, and as we climbed, we heard, louder and louder, the clatter of the teletype machine. The place was deserted, and the man on duty sat at his desk at the back of the room, poring over charts and graphs. He rose and came toward us. On and on went the teletype, rattling out its coded story of the skies, the story that is never done. From it rolled out endless coils of yellow paper, which fell in curves and waves onto the floor. It would stop, pause as if to catch its breath, and then start again with fresh energy and clatter, steadily and yet hurriedly recording the conditions of the night. No one had read the coiled papers; they lay in orderly disarray on the floor where they had fallen, full of useless information. Now, as we told the man what we needed, he moved to it, and picking up the yellow papers, he hunted with his finger down a long list to find the latest of the local reports. Suddenly the machine became personal, of vital importance. It was reporting for us, for our flight. He tore off a sheet and brought it to us, and I read the code as he talked. Clear, perfect weather at Gordonsville and Pulaski, two stations that were, I knew, deep in the Virginia mountains; I saw, as I read, the loneliness and the moonlight on the great slopes, and the reflections on the wet precipices near the summits. Clear also at Raleigh-Durham, where the airport lies midway in the plain between the towns. Richmond, Charlotte; all the same, clear and cold, an extensive high-pressure system. As I read, I felt myself relax; we nodded to each other in agreement, for we had already made our plans. Frederick would fly and I would navigate, and if, when we reached our home airport with its unlighted runways, we did not like what we saw, we could always go on to the big field, where there are lights. Standing there with the yellow coded sheets before me, I read on, idly, down the list to the reports of faraway places which meant nothing to me; at least, I thought, not tonight. There, CHA . . . Chattanooga . . . estimated ceiling 800 feet, visibility one mile, sleet showers, temperature 32° dew point 31°, wind NW at 27 knots, barometer 29.92 and falling . . . so I decoded. And I felt my guts tighten, by proxy this time, for men flying in that stuff.

"Better weather east than over the mountains," said the weatherman. "That front will be in here tomorrow noon." He was polite, and wished us a pleasant trip. Another sort of remoteness replaced that which divided us from our friends; this time it was the remoteness of routine. We said goodbye.

We walked out to the Stinson, squatting there fat

and black in the cold night. No trace could be seen now of its red, rich finish, but it glistened as it caught the moon and the many colored lights of the buildings and the tower. I touched the tail, and my hand left a mark; it was wet with dew. We untied it, and I wrapped my coat around me as I settled inside, and threw my hat, with a sigh of pleasure, into the seat behind me. The instrument panel glowed softly as Frederick snapped the switches, and the little red and green navigation lights shone on the wing tips. The plane moved slowly forward while Frederick spoke with the tower, and I collected my charts. We were on concrete, and there were lights, widely spaced, all around us in the darkness. Lights, bewildering lights were everywhere, scattered in every direction. The entangled runways and taxiways, the narrow ribbons which had confused us so in full daylight, were utterly enmeshed with one another now, and we could see no lines of lights, no pattern to guide us.

"Flash your landing light," said the tower. "Now I have you in sight. Bear to the left and then straight ahead." Slowly we moved on, and a light, low on the ground, passed close under a wing. What was there? Concrete or muddy grass? We felt our way slowly.

"Is your heading three two?" said the tower, and at that moment I felt a lurch as a wheel slipped off the concrete into the mud. The engine roared as Frederick opened the throttle, but we were trapped.

"Is your heading three two? Taxi straight ahead," repeated the tower. We climbed out and shoved and lifted as my elegant heels sank deeper at every step, till at last we were free. Frederick got in and I stayed out to guide him, but as he started to taxi the wheel slipped again. The plane jumped forward as he gunned it, spattering me with mud! Then we were taxiing on firm concrete, and at last we reached the end of the runway, and we turned. Now I could see ahead into the distance, where the lights were red and green in dense patches.

"Stinson three two Kilo, is your heading two twelve?" said the tower. "You are cleared for take-off." A take-off into that mess of lights? A take-off of faith? The tower can see us, so it must be all right; we just keep straight toward those green lights and pray we don't hit the mud. I held on to the strut as we gained speed, and as soon as we rose from the concrete the lights became orderly, outlining the paths of the airport as a clear geometrical design. I breathed deeply as the bunches of colored lights flashed below the wings and we passed over the boundary, and deeper yet as we turned back toward the city we had left, with its diamond chains spread out in all directions, thousands of pin points of lights. The air was smooth; the turbulence from the currents which rise from the sun-warmed earth had gone as the sun set, and no ripples moved.

"Heading?" said Frederick. I had forgotten about that! I was on duty now and I wrenched my mind from the transformed city below. "Sixty-five," I told him, pulling a number out of my memory, where I had stored it for just such a moment. Then, to be sure, I checked the chart and as usual I noted the time.

The air was thick as the Stinson climbed through it.

Cold air is dense and heavy, and I could feel the bite of the wings, as they rode on it, and up. Presently we were high enough. Frederick leveled off, trimmed it carefully, and turned it loose. I could see over the nose now, and there was a group of lights just ahead of us; then they were under us, and then behind, and then quickly lost. We hung in space, motionless, while the towns slid under us. We were over a huge revolving globe. There was no sound in the steady engine roar, no movement in our flight. We hovered in a world of lights. Above us was the moon; below, the many-colored lamps moved as we sat there, still, in the softly illuminated cockpit. A town some thirty miles away, which is usually invisible in haze on the southern horizon, was clear now in the distance, outlined by many tiny chains of twinkling lights, more delicate than filigree of gold.

The moon dimmed all but the brightest stars, and as our eyes became accustomed to the dark, we began to see the ground almost as well as in daylight. The woods and fields were clearly defined, and although on the roads the cars themselves were not visible, each one projected a moving oval of light which traveled ahead of it. There was a train with a huge searchlight, and water that reflected it as it passed over a bridge. So we flew, sitting close together, holding hands in the little cabin, fingers interlocked. We were warm in the cold night and safe in the gentle glow of the panel lights, and too soon we were home. We could see the airport and the hangar, and the floodlights were full on; perhaps someone was working on his plane. Frederick made a long, wide pattern and a long approach, feeling his way down, power on, nose high, like landing on water. The hangar lights guided us, and Frederick lit the powerful landing beam that is on the leading edge of the wing. For a moment I was lost, blinking at the illuminated circle that was the propeller, and then I saw grass tufts flashing by, and the wheels touched, and we were down. The spell was broken.

CHAPTER 7

All over the land, there are airports; places, that is, where an airplane can find its way down and onto a reasonably smooth surface; where it can divest itself of its flying speed and sit upon the ground again. A place of refuge from the storm, perhaps, or a source of fuel, or just a place to buy an ice-cream cone; all of them the same yet different, and all of them important. They range from the smallest, roughest hillside strips to the enormous commercial and military fields, of all sizes and shapes. There are private strips at the back yards of farmhouses, sometimes marked on the charts for emergency use but often hidden among the wheat and cattle fields, so that only the local pilots know of their existence. Then there are those on the outskirts of towns, usually operated for profit; and the municipal ones. During the war, many concrete strips were built by the military and have since been deserted. Some have been reactivated, but others have gradually decayed, and the frost and the weeds have broken up the hard surface until these fields have become useless. At the largest airports, the commercial fields, many planes take off and land every minute, and then there are the huge Air Force bases, forbidden to civilian pilots . . . and who, except in distress, wouldn't avoid them anyway?

Of airports, I like ours the best, but I like them all, and sometimes I fly to the big commercial ones to enjoy watching the double life that goes on there. Outside the terminal building, the airliners, the buses of the sky, routinely collect and deposit passengers. Beautiful silvery things, however easily they come and go, they are celestial creatures from which the miraculous has not quite been stripped away. Inside, more routine. Here, captains and co-pilots wander, uniformed and glamorous: the few, among the many. At the other side of a big airport, little known to many of the people who use the terminal, are the privately owned planes, and the offices and repair shops. An instructor or two will be there, ready to give lessons; planes can be rented, and transient aircraft tied down safely for the night.

The traffic-control tower plays the part of Master of

Ceremonies, and co-ordinates the airport into a unit. It issues instructions both to airliners and to the smallest planes for take-offs, landings and ground movements, and traffic at some places is sufficient to require a separate radio channel for taxiing operations. Mainly, the function of the tower is that of the policeman at the crossroads, enormously complicated by three dimensions instead of two, by the essential differences among Cubs, DC-7s and jets, by weather and other matters.

For traffic on its way from one place to another, there are the Airways Communication Centers, which are located at or near the big airports. These keep in radio communication with pilots flying in instrument weather, to avoid collisions and to enable them to navigate. They operate the radio beams and other, newer types of radio-navigation aids, and it is to them, not to the towers, that we talk on our cross-country flights when we need weather information, or to report our progress if we have filed a Flight Plan. Under normal conditions, these two services are most proficient and pleasant, and they do much to make flying safer. In emergencies, many lives have been saved by them, through radioed instructions to planes lost above or in an overcast, to desperate pilots who find themselves in a mess, with gas supply dwindling, and nowhere to turn to find a way down.

We, who are licensed to fly only under Visual Flight Rules, are free to wander where we please. We may, if we wish, follow the airways, the air roads used by commercial traffic, or we may fly, as the crow is supposed to do, in a straight line from one place to another. We may, if we wish, file a Flight Plan, but for local flights over populated country we do not do this. We just take off and go, and we call the tower at our destination when we are a few miles away, and receive instructions for landing. The two-way radio procedure, which at first seemed to complicate the already-difficult life of a beginner, seems now very useful. Not only is it a safeguard against possible collision in the crowded air, but also it gives valuable information concerning wind, barometric pressure (otherwise altitude) and other matters which influence the approach and landing. Aircraft carrying these radios are classified as broadcasting stations, and, minuscule though they be, are subject to elaborate registration and inspection by the Federal Communications Commission. When flying such an airplane, the pilot must carry a radio operator's license, third class. A knowledge of the Morse code is not required to obtain one of these, neither is there any qualifying examination. The pilot, on payment of a small fee, collects yet another card to add to the accumulation of licenses in his wallet and that is all. As far as I know, there is no fourth class.

Many of the trainer planes, the Cubs and Aeroncas, do not carry radios, and for them a system of contact with the tower is established by means of signals. The light gun is used, with brightly colored lights down at the end of a long tube. This device can be pointed from the tower toward the airplane, and is not visible to other craft. By suitable red or green lights the tower can, in some measure, direct the pilot, and the pilot, by his actions, indicates his intentions to the tower. As he flies in the pattern, he rocks his wings to acknowledge his receipt of the code signal. Although it is better than nothing, the arrangement, as can well be imagined, is liable to serious breakdown of communication, and it is going out of use at the busiest airports, which now require a two-way radio for aircraft using the field.

The signal code is simple; among some eight variations of steady or flashing lights, there is one, alternating flashes of green and red, which means "Exercise extreme caution," or "Be on the alert for hazardous conditions." I have only seen this once, quite unexpectedly. Red and green, the tower flashed at me, as I flew into the pattern; red and green! I wiggled my wings in acknowledgement and I puzzled. What could be on their minds, the minds of those tiny figures high in their glass dome? How does one exercise extreme caution when one sees no threat, no enemy? Whatever enemy it is, I thought, it is not invincible, for the tower *could* tell me to go away; a flashing red light —airport unsafe, do not land—and that, it had not done. Everything looked normal. Other traffic? Balloons or dirigibles, which have the right-of-way? I looked carefully all around, and craned my neck to see as much as possible into the blind spot below and under my tail. Holes in the runway? No, there was no white cross painted on the concrete, the sign that the strip was unfit for use. Whirlwinds? Little tornadoes in the air? Impossible, I knew, on a day like this, with a high, unbroken overcast. Moreover, I had flown in from a nearby airport, and the wind was gentle, almost calm. I had noted the wind tee, and was landing the way it indicated. The skin of my back began to tingle at the thought of the ambush that was awaiting me. I opened the throttle, climbed, and circled the field a second time, and when I came around and back down for the approach, there it was again, red and green, flashing the warning! I became mildly indignant. It would be foolish, I decided, to go home without landing, and never find out what was the matter. So I continued the glide, watchful, tense, ready at any moment to push the throttle and get out. I landed, and nothing happened. The tower flashed its light at me, green now with permission to taxi. I went at once to the nearest telephone, and a confidential gentleman told me that the bearings of the wind indicator needed oil, and it had stuck, indicating, fortunately, the runway in use!

I remember another breakdown, a much worse one. I had flown the Aeronca over to meet a friend, and, with an hour to spare, I telephoned the tower for permission to circle, practicing "touch-and go" landings. Instead of a gradual loss of speed and a complete stop after touchdown, the throttle is opened just after the wheels are on the ground and another take-off is made at once. The student gets much more landing practice this way, for he loses no time in taxiing, and the runway is cleared for other traffic. Sometimes on the approach to an airport the tower will tell you "The Cub on final will make a touch-and-go landing. You are second to land." And you plan your approach accordingly. That day there was not much traffic, said the tower, and I had their permission. So I worked and worked, and always, as I flew down wind in the pattern, the green light from the tower shone on schedule. Eventually my time was up. Once more round, I decided, and that would be the last. I looked around me for traffic, and saw my green light, and came down on the runway, and as I slowed to a stop I heard a roaring like a herd of angry lions behind me. I crouched low, helpless, and over my little Aeronca came a huge shadow, followed a moment later by the monstrous body of an airliner, shuddering with fury as it climbed. I had made him go round! As I taxied to the hangar I tried to fortify myself, and prepare answers to all the nasty things the tower would say to me, but they never even telephoned. It was not really my fault, nor was it theirs! I preferred not to meet the captain of the airliner, so I timed my take-off carefully, after the liner had landed, and before he reached the ramp. I wished I had a radio.

The radio which came with the Stinson when we bought it was a good one, but like all low-frequency receivers, it suffered from attacks of ill-humor during summer thunder weather, when it would crackle and buzz, so much so that sometimes I could not interpret the tower's instructions. The fear of doing the wrong thing made me quite shy of the big airports, and I would fly nearby, and listen for a time to the chattering of the tower directing traffic, before I dared press the transmitter button, and talk. Once, I remember, my courage failed me, and I flew back home. Sometimes I would speak gently into that marvelous contraption, the mike, holding it close to my lips. "This is Stinson three two kilo," and the tower would hear a voice out of the sky, a disembodied voice, without direction; a voice like the shout of the cuckoo, flat and toneless. "Five miles east at two thousand. Landing instructions, please." "Three two kilo," the reply would come, followed by a flood of details of wind, barometer and other matters. "Land on runway two six. I have you in sight. Call me on base." "Roger." Glide, lose altitude, down wind, and turn on the base leg. I hear the tower talking to someone else, and it is no use to call till he has finished. I wait. "Bonanza ten zero victor, you are cleared to enter the pattern." It is now that I wish for extra hands. Right hand on the throttle, left on the wheel, and the contraption is on my lap, its string twisted around my knee. However did it get that way? Somehow I disentangle it, and in doing so I let go of the wheel, and the nose rises. I push forward and struggle some more. Now I have it, contraption held firmly on top of the wheel, both together in one hand, throttle in the other. Then, reaching forward with my lips to confide in it, I lean my weight on the wheel and the airplane dives. Finally I get it trimmed, and I wonder: What do the tower boys think I am doing? Am I having an emergency, or just playing roller coaster? I hear the welcome words, "You are cleared to land," and now my affair with the tower is over. "Roger," I reply, and now I can devote all my attention to landing, and it had better be a good one. It will be right under them, and they will watch with interest, for they saw the antics, and they know that the pilot is a woman. But unless there is a crisis, they won't call me again. The Bonanza is on base now, somewhere behind me. A wheel landing, and I am on. I call once more for permission to taxi.

This method of communication works well most of

the time, and the tower and the pilot understand each other. Once in a while, though, the unexpected happens. The time, for instance, when I had three passengers with me, an unusually heavy load, which changes considerably the glide and landing behavior of the Stinson. The final clearance had been given and acknowledged, and all was well. Just as I touched, close beside the tower, a great noise came over the earphones, a sudden, urgent voice. The cry of "Three two Kilo" shattered my ears and my security. For God's sake there must be something awfully wrong! An airliner on my tail? Better get out of here, at once! I did the only thing I knew to do, I jammed the throttle forward till it touched the firewall, and leaned my weight on the wheel to prevent a stall as the nose came up, extra high because of the load in the back seat. We were air-borne again, out of danger. The voice finished, "You are cleared to land."

At our home, though, the Airport-on-the-Hill, these aspects of air life are missing, and are replaced by others. There is no tower, so pilots, landing or on the ground, keep a careful watch for other traffic. No airliners use the field and there are no planes for rent, and no facilities other than an office and a telephone, and gasoline. Once a year or so (a matter of comment from everyone) a DC-3 will land there, making gigantic tracks in the sod, clearly visible from the air for months. There, days may go by in bad weather without anyone opening the hangar doors, and then, on fine weekends, every one of the airplanes will be out on pleasure trips to the beach or the mountains, leaving behind an empty, desolate barn. At sundown they return, are fitted into their special places, and the doors are closed. There are no runway lights, and little night flying. Sometimes a pilot will plan to start cross country at the first streak of dawn, and will check and gas his plane the evening before, and leave it ready. More often, in the early morning the caretaker is asleep in the little house and nothing disturbs the wide grass prairie except a bird or two, calling to each other, or a rabbit, hopping about in the patches of clover, leaving its tracks in the dew.

One morning, in early summer, the ghastly cry of a screech owl jolted me from half sleep to full awakening. Frederick was out of town and I was alone in the house, which is set in a grove of pines. Often, I listen at night to their gentle gossiping, or, in gusty weather, to the tugging, heart-rending sound as the wind pulls at the thousands of clusters of needles, which bend and twist as they cling to the trees. Or, on very still nights, I can hear a faint and delicate hissing sound, continuous in the quietness; pine needles falling onto the carpet below. These noises, and the creaks and groans of the woodwork are always much louder on the rare nights when Frederick is away, so that I sleep lightly and wake early. And maybe it was nothing but a screech owl, nothing else than a soft-flying bird out hunting, that wakened me, but the cries of the strangled children of the ages are concentrated in the noise, and after that, sleep is impossible. I crept down the stairs feeling strangely guilty, as if in danger of discovery. I grabbed some bread and milk and ran out into the cold, washed air of the before-dawn hour. The east was already faintly golden as I started the car and drove through wisps of vapor to the airport. There was no one to be seen. I crept down the steps and crouched in the dew and grass beside the hangar door. Reaching under it with my fingers, I worked at the great pin which holds the lock until I could raise it, and the door was loose and could be pushed back. The opening of the heavy metal door on its iron runners is always noisy, but this morning it shrieked and howled, a match for the screech owl itself! The whole village will come out, I thought, running with dogs and guns to see what is making such a noise. At least the caretaker will be aroused, and come down, probably in his pajamas. But to my joy, no one came. I waited until the echoes died away, and I took the wooden chocks from under the wheels of the Aeronca, and allowed it to roll out of the hangar. I checked it; it was all in order, and I replaced the chocks for starting it. The world was still too dark to see the end of the runway, so I sat there awhile in the chill dawn and waited, watching the slowly increasing light, hoping to take off just before the sun came, so that I could see it rise as I gained altitude. Two rabbits came, and watched me suspiciously while they ate. I shivered, not with cold, but because, incredibly, I was sitting there by myself, with an airplane of my own, and I was able to take it into the sky and go, anywhere I pleased.

It was very quiet, but light enough now. Still no one came. I stood in the dew and pulled the propeller; the Aeronca burst into life. Watchful of the whirring and almost invisible blades, I removed the wheel chocks and climbed in, and as I fastened the safety belt I taxied out and away from the hangar. The wheels kicked up sprays of dew from the grass onto the undersurface of the wings. I took off and rose into silky smoothness, not a ripple or a breath of air disturbed my wings. The aroma of the morning was strong and sweet. The village street lights glittered, and the hills were dark and clear. The eastern sky was glowing with the hidden fire below the horizon, and the fire was reflected in the dozens of farmyard ponds which are scattered over the land. I looked closely at the ponds, puzzled, for each had something hanging over it, a small pink crown. Then, as I gained altitude and flew over one of them, I saw that it was a ring of mist rising from the surface of the water in a perfect doughnut shape, which coiled up and rose from the center outward, like a smoke ring blown from gigantic lips. They were everywhere; each pond was lidded with its own pink doughnut, all at the same height, each fitted in size to its pond, and all rising up into the air. Then the sun came, jumping over the edge of the world, and a moment later a ray shot across the land, throwing shadows as it went. All at once the doughnuts changed color, and were now white against the dark blue hills. While I circled and watched, they rose quickly as the warmth of the sun fell upon them. They broke up into fragments and faded away, and were gone.

The village lights were turned off now. The twin chimneys on the riverbank belched up black smoke. Someone down there was firing the furnaces, I supposed. Two graceful plumes rose together into the quiet sky, and together they curved sideways and drifted in the pressure of the light wind. I flew westward toward the river, where I could see a cloud layer, low down. At about fifteen hundred feet it spread across the marshes and over the farm land, a very thin layer, only a few feet thick, but mottled with clear places, so that as I flew above it I could get glimpses of the farms below. I nosed the plane down through a hole, and flew below for a while, then up again through another hole, then down. In and out I went, sewing stitches in the cloud. What was I doing? Did anyone guess the fun I was having? An idiot dolphin, gamboling in the sky? I laughed on my way back to the airport, and came down low to land. There on the grass were the tracks of my take-off run, still visible in the dew. I could see clearly where I had taxied and turned, and where the tracks ended as the wheels left the ground. I landed very carefully, with quite unnecessary precision, using the throttle so that I touched again in the very spot where the take-off run had ended. I had completed the circle of my little journey. There on the steps stood the caretaker, wondering. All the rest of the day I kept thinking of my flight, and smiling to myself.

Many times since the flight of the doughnuts I have taken off in the early morning, either to go somewhere, or just for fun. Almost always it is quiet, the air of heavy, rich quality, and sometimes strange and wonderful things are to be seen in the dawn sky. I have seen the mist over the ponds in corkscrews, spiraling upward, and once I found a delicate membrane of cloud, infinitely thin and fragile, a sort of skin. Once, a little blob of vapor came sailing by, a little sphere a yard or so across, all by itself. And there is always peace, and freedom and loneliness, in the morning sky.

There was one morning, though, when things were different. The hangar was wide open before the dawn, and the lights were blazing. There was an unusual feeling of excitement. An annular eclipse of the sun was to take place that day, very early. The sun was expected to rise already partly hidden, and the cocks were scheduled to crow once, and go back to bed. We hoped to see it from high up, and we promised a group of local astronomers, and our daughter, places in the airplanes. I would fly her, and my husband would take the astronomers in the Stinson.

We had wakened that morning while it was still dark, and there were no stars. We drove through fog, right to the ground, most of the way to the airport; but as we got near, the stuff began to break up, with layers remaining in the hollows. The big plain of the airport seemed clear in the dimness, with some little wisps of mist, barely waist-high, rising from the damp ground. Several planes were already parked on the apron. We sorted out three young men from the group which was waiting, and the others went off to watch from an easterly prominence on a hill. We checked and started the airplanes. A Beechcraft loaded with men and elaborate cameras took off as we were warming up, and disappeared. As I looked around to follow him, I saw that the end of the runway had vanished, hidden in a layer of fog. I stopped my engine and got out and ran to the Stinson.

"The field's closing in . . . we'd better wait awhile, hadn't we?"

"Yes, wait! It'll clear soon. This is just morning stuff."

But the astronomers were anxious not to miss the sunrise, and just then there came a hole; the Stinson took off through it and was gone. I wished that he had waited. I shouldn't worry, though, I thought; he has gas for four hours and a good radio. He can look after himself. But I was lonely, knowing what might happen if the fog closed in. And there was the child, up so early to see the show, pouting disapproval at being grounded by a fussy mother. Gas I had, but no radio in the little trainer, no way to go if caught above that nasty mess. But as I hesitated, the fog cleared again and I took off, intent on staying very close to the airport, so that I could get down at once, if I wanted. And then, as we rose off the ground, the windshield clouded completely over; the world was gone! I pulled the window open, pulled on the carbureter heat control and shoved the nose down, all in one instant. Through the open window I could see clearly, the sky and the layers of fog and the village steeples. The windshield cleared as I turned back and found the airport, and we flew toward the rising sun. Then we saw a divided world. The sun was over the fog bank, which was sharp-edged like a precipice. The top was rolling and shiny, clean and fair like untouched snow, and solid as far as I could see. Somewhere in the gloom underneath it was our home. Westward, the country was open, and I could see that the hills were clothed in veils and scarves of mist. The child behind me gasped as she saw the sun, partly eclipsed, through her smoked glasses. I noted carefully the exact position of that menacing wall, ready to run for home if it should start to move our way. But there was no wind to blow it, and as it stayed, I gained courage. I saw the small, red Stinson far above us, also, I felt, watching. . . . I edged up to the precipice, even over it, and let the wheels of the trainer dangle in the snowy layer. If only one could land, and walk around on it, and feel it . . . it looked more solid than water, with the gear stirring ripples that ruffled the shiny surface.

It never got really dark, above the fog bank. Back and forth we flew, till the moon moved on and the sun emerged, fully bright. Down to a landing, the Stinson close behind us. Comments, thanks, promises of photographs, all very polite, with the faint lack of comprehension of the non-pilot. The unfortunates on the hilltop had seen nothing, for their view had been completely cut off by the fog. A fine spectacle, said our three, as they folded their cameras. With thanks again they went off. We went home, too, plunging through the fog to a second breakfast of coffee and sugar buns.

Saturday and Sunday afternoons are the times of greatest activity at the Airport-on-the-Hill. Young men, with their girls sitting close beside them, will park their cars on the high ground near the office, overlooking the runways. Small boys with bicycles ride out from the village, up the hill, and they lean up against the railings, under the big notice which reads, "No admittance without a permit." Presently two or three of a group will ease themselves under the fence, or halfway down the steps, gradually moving closer, the boldest first. Usually they get chased out before they reach the hangar, for they may, in ignorance, damage the fragile aircraft. They pull propellers, or climb onto the struts and crawl onto the wings in their efforts to see inside, and the toe of a small boot can easily crash through fabric, or make a dent in skin-stressed metal fuselage.

To forestall such trouble, and because boys like airplanes, I invite them to look around and even to sit at the controls. I show them, for instance, how backward movement of the stick makes the elevators tilt up, and the airflow which catches on them forces the tail down, and the nose rises. "That's a fine jet job," said a small boy to his big brother, as he pointed to the old Aeronca trainer, and he asked me, "Can you drive it?" I told him yes, I could, and explained briefly the difference between propeller-driven and jet aircraft. I knew ahead of time what the next question would be. "How much do you charge for a ride?" I told them that I did not charge for rides, but that, if anyone brought me written permission from his parents, I would take him up with me. As the result of this policy, I have a collection of notes, written often with obvious difficulty, in pencil, on odd scraps of paper. By the time they are handed over to me, on a note of triumph and with assurance that I will now fulfill my part of the bargain, they are often hard to decipher, crumpled and moist from their contact with grubby pockets. One note, written on a blank sheet from a waitress's order pad, read: "Ed may ride in the ladies airplane but I don't like it." I took Ed for a very short flight, and I was glad when we landed. Another note, permission to fly once, on a specified date, was erased and altered by the time I got it.

Joe, I think, met with a lot of family opposition, for day after day he would be at the airport, explaining that tomorrow he would have the note, for sure. Finally he won out. Proudly he handed over his note, and soon he was sitting in the Stinson beside me, bright-eyed with anticipation. But he sat silent, in spite of all the switches and dials on the instrument panel, and he asked none of the usual questions. At last, as we taxied down the runway, I asked, "Isn't there anything you want to know, before we take off?" "Yes," he said. "What does it feel like, to be in the air?"

We flew, over his home and school, and all around and down again. He thanked me most politely, pushed a dollar bill into my hand, and ran. I have not seen him since, and had no chance to find out how he felt in the air.

Johnny, on the other hand, is a dedicated airman. He is a sturdy twelve-year-old, calm and determined. He knows how to get the airplanes in and out of the hangar, exactly when to pull a chock out from under a wheel, and when to push or to hold back. He counts it a privilege to be allowed to clean the oil stains from under the belly of a fuselage. He is always there at the right moment, but never underfoot, and by sheer persistent, pleasant helpfulness he wangles rides out of everyone. Every few weeks he will sit in the Aeronca, propped up with cushions, convincing himself that he is nearer to the great day when he will be able to reach the rudder pedals. I hope, one day, I'll teach Johnny to fly.

Albert is jolly and enormously fat. His eyes and teeth

are gleaming white and his skin is very black. High up in the air in the Stinson, I give him the sign that he has the controls. This is his moment. He hauls back with all his might on the wheel and then suddenly lets go, whooping with glee at the roller-coaster effect. He is specially delighted if he has a buddy in the rear seat. Grinning all over his flat face, he turns round after each oscillation, to make sure we are all as happy as he is. Albert knows a lot about planes, too, and on the rare occasions when he happens to want, he can fly straight and level as well as any of us.

One day we landed the Aeronca dead stick. The engine had been running perfectly, with no indication of trouble. Fortunately, we were right over the airport, and had plenty of altitude when it happened. There was no warning; it just stopped as it idled, and there was the propeller, standing up in front of us. It all seemed so calm and natural.

I said, "I'll take it." "Let me!" pleaded my companion, and he landed it, and let it run on toward the hangar as far as it would go. As we came to a stop and got out to push, he asked me if I had cut the switch on purpose, to see what he would do. Then we found ourselves in the center of a group of men, all interested in the landing and eager with suggestions. We took off the engine cowling, and, trying to look wise, we peeked and peered inside. We pulled the propeller and could find nothing wrong. So we started it, and it ran, but with a peculiar hissing, sucking sound, and then it hesitated and stopped. Finally we found the trouble—a broken primer line, which allowed air to enter the carbureter through the break, like the breathing of a man with a hole in his chest. We repaired the line and the engine ran smoothly again.

On Saturday morning early, I started it up. I checked it with extra care and could find no fault with it. So I took off, alone, for the cross-country trip to the mechanic, to get a new primer line installed. The morning air was thick. No waves, no ripples even, and the little ship seemed to swim in a quiet sea. I took up my compass course and listened to the steady firing of the cylinders. I trimmed the plane carefully to fly straight and level, and I thought I could see, in that still air, the very slightly different angle at which the wings are set, in order to counteract the torque of the spinning propeller. I held the stick between my knees, folded my hands, and contrasted my situation happily with that of a driver of a car on the highway below. I pitied him, down there imprisoned among the trees and the stones, and I ran a few circles round him, just for fun, and went on my way.

Then I began to fret. The firing seemed to roughen. Everything is all right, I told myself. It is just plain stupid to get tense and fussy, when yesterday's trouble has been found and fixed. One can hear all sorts of strange things, especially when one is listening for them; all sorts of small changes in the quality of the noise, which really take place inside one's head. Then the engine popped and spluttered, the tachometer needle swayed crazily, and we began going down. I did all I could. I picked out the best-looking field, and remembered that there was no wind. Land uphill, then, if possible. And as I pumped the throttle, the engine caught again, and slowly the plane regained the five hundred feet it had lost. For a while all seemed well, and I had time to reconsider the driver of the car. Undoubtedly a sensible fellow, on his way to a routine job after a breakfast of fried eggs and coffee. If I had to land this damned thing in a field, perhaps he would give me a lift into town. Then the hiccups began again, worse than before, and I lost altitude fast. I chose a landing place and planned my approach. Then the engine picked up once more. At last, with deep relief, I saw the airport in the distance. I had begun to hope that I could make it, when a flash of light above the hangar caught my eye. I looked carefully, desperately, and saw an orange rotating beacon, the signal of limited visibility, too low for flight under ordinary contact rules. With such a signal, landing is forbidden for my plane, which has no radio equipment, and there it was, flashing its message to me, from ten miles away! In this perfect weather, whatever emergency had they there? Was it safe to land, I wondered, if ever I got there? I had my own private emergency, and no mean one either, and the nearest alternate airport was miles away, and the fields below me now were very rough. After one more bout of hiccups I was over the hangar. Looking down from six hundred feet, I could see no cause for trouble, and the buildings, airplanes and cars seemed to be in order. No one was running anywhere. I circled once, hesitating, and then I saw a small plane coming to land, and thankfully I followed him. Tired out and very puzzled, I taxied to the shop, cut the ailing engine, and walked up the steps to the weather station. The operator turned at the sound of the door.

"I'm glad you came in," he said. "I have some tomato plants I saved for you." I leaned against the door while I collected my wits.

"What is the idea," I said slowly, "of that rotating beacon?"

"Oh!" he said. "I forgot it. We had some fog here, a while back."

That day there were no cars in the parking place, and the doors of the hangar were tight shut. The gale had forced the wind sock out straight and held it there, and the tip moved gently around like an elephant's trunk, stretched out peanut hunting. Riding up and down on it was a small dark bird. My student Don and I leaned against the west wind as we went down the steps to the hangar and opened the sliding door just enough to squeeze inside, and shut it behind us. The gusty wind, which could not reach us now, rattled and banged on the metal roof. Then it was quiet and we could talk, while we waited for the next blast. Then, wham . . . again and again.

We settled ourselves to the job of removing the wheel covers (pants, we call them) from the Stinson, which had a flat tire. Flying was impossible anyway, for no one could taxi a light plane in that wind. It would be turned over, or blown off the runway into the trees. Crash, rattle, bang, went the roof again. Presently, as we were lying on the concrete floor trying to reach the bolts, the attendant came down from the office, and as he greeted us, the telephone rang. "No," he answered. "Nothing's landed here." He came toward us, frowning. "The boy at the filling station up the road. He says he saw a plane go down over the hill. That's the second time he's called. A silver plane, low-winged, he says." A queer tale, I thought, but little boys do see and hear strange things. Probably nothing in it. Low-winged, silver . . . an Ercoupe, possibly. And, yes, I thought with rising distress, that direction *is* down wind from the runway. Anything trying to reach the field would be over that way today, for sure. And that is the worst terrain around here, too; no fields anywhere, just miles and miles of rocky woodland. But flying . . . on such a day? With a wind of forty knots or more? It didn't make sense, but still I fretted. The Stinson tire could wait. Why not go and talk to the boy, at least?

So we took Don's green Chevrolet, Don and the airport attendant and I, and soon, as we listened to the boy, the story gained credence and my distress increased. Engine? No, he hadn't heard one. Large and silver, the thing had come low overhead, and seemed to turn behind the bunch of trees on the far hill, and then he had heard a crash. That was all, and that, I knew, was just what could happen after an engine failure, on a day like this. Blown too far out on the down-wind leg, had the pilot tried to make a steep turn back toward the field and safety, only to undershoot the runway and make a forced landing in the treetops? Or had a gust hit him, and made him stall and spin? So we consulted. How could we find it, if there really were a plane down in the forest? The Stinson? It had a flat tire. But we could, I felt, make a gesture, for the sake of peace of mind. And dressed in overalls and heavy shoes, I was ready to enjoy a scramble over rocks and across streambeds, on a wild afternoon in January, just before spring. But I sensed that Don felt differently. He is a very practical person, of wide experience, and one to be relied on in an emergency. He is an athlete, too, and a woodsman, and I think he could see no use in the three of us searching the woods. A plane, buried in the thick trees, would be well hidden, and could be bypassed only a few yards away. But he made no protest, and, feeling rather foolish, I asked him to drive along the dirt track, as far as the car could go. Then we separated, and walked out fanwise. I walked directly toward the bunch of trees, whose position we noted over the next ridge. The airport attendant went to my right, and Don strode away down the creek to my left. We were to meet where the road crossed another, a couple of miles away. I worked my way into the valley and came to the creek. It was larger than I had thought, and I had to hunt for a place to cross over, by jumping from one huge boulder to another. On the other side I ran up the hill, climbing and scrambling. I peered from side to side, but I could see so small an area in the woods; anyway I kept looking, without very much idea of what I might see. I went on, getting lonely now, and thinking what a crazy thing this was that we were doing. The wind was dying, the gusts were further apart now, and at the hilltop I found a small clearing, waist-high with stiff weeds, and an over-grown cart track which led through a gap in the trees. Through it, far away in the distance, I could see the hangar

and the end of the runway. Two or perhaps three miles, I
supposed. I crossed the track and plunged on into the
forest, feeling less alone now that I knew where I was, and
enjoying the delicate smell of incipient growth which rose
up from the leaves and moss as I crushed them. Down hill
I went now, over or around huge grey rocks, and as I came
to a tiny waterway I heard faintly, between the gusts, Don's
voice. "Hallo!" "Hallo!" I answered in the next pause,
and "Hallo! Come down the hill!" he called. I struggled
through the underbrush, guided by his voice, till I saw
him, standing high (how strange!) on a pile of tin cans?
. . . a garbage dump? . . . a mass of twisted metal . . .
a wing . . . an airplane! And as he reached out his hand
and pulled me up beside him, I saw that a large tree trunk,
sheared off by a wing, had fallen across the fuselage,
which lay on some rocks; the tail hung over them, out of
sight. It was quiet there, absolutely quiet. Automatically I
sniffed for gasoline . . . there was none. I looked down,
and at my feet, embedded in the wreckage, I saw the tops
of two brown heads, bare and low in the crushed cockpits.
Shocked and speechless, we stood there on the broken
wing. Then the head in the rear cockpit groaned, and I
reached down, and gently touched the stiff hair, close to
my feet. "How's my buddy?" it said, and then, pleading,
"Get me out of here." I could not see his face, for his
shoulders were hunched forward by the weight of his parachute. We pulled it up, and I slipped a torn branch beneath
it, so that he raised his face, and it was bloody. The head
in the front cockpit sank lower, and moaned, too.

"Don! My God, Don! What *do* we do?" Get them out, with only our bare hands to tear at the metal, and lay them, bleeding, on the rocks? Get help, ambulance and doctor? That was the only way. Telephone? Yes, there was one at the filling station. How to get help into that wilderness? Don would go back to the car, telephone and drive slowly toward town, along the road. I would go down the track I had seen, toward the airport, and hope to find a way in. It would have to be that way, no one could bring an ambulance the way I had come. We must both go, and leave the heads, alone and helpless. We could do nothing else. We could not help them, if we stayed. Somehow, I hated to go. But there was no other way, so I touched the stiff hair again and hoped he would understand. "Listen!" I said, loudly and definitely. "We are going to get help. We'll be back and get you out, very soon!" And I ran off. I ran and ran and scrambled through the tall, dry weeds, and ran some more, up the hill. I thought of what was below the heads. My stomach rose and I went to the ditch and vomited, and ran on. Where the track turned, I made a mistake, and tried to find a short cut by forcing my way through some brambles, but I had to turn back. After that, I ran round the curves. I ran through a deserted farmyard and past a pigsty, where I missed my footing in the high weeds and fell headlong into a mess of cockleburs. Finally, choking and gasping for breath, I reached the road just as Don drove up. He had telephoned and help was on the way. Nothing to do now, but get one's breath and wait. I leaned against his car, and my hand shook as I tried to tidy my hair. I carefully picked off some of the cockleburs, one by one, from my overalls. How lucky, I thought, that they are not in my hair! How difficult it was to get hold of them, with my fingers shaking so! Don talked while I gasped. He had got tired of walking in the woods, and on a sudden hunch, he had climbed the stem of a tall, thin tree for a better look round. And from there he had seen the wreck, just a telltale glint of metal, catching the sun on the slope below. My chest hurt, and still I gasped.

Presently we saw the ambulance, red lights flashing far down the road. Don went with it, and I waited for the doctor, who came a few moments later. I thought: God help me, suppose I can't find the way. But I led him straight through and into the wilderness, with his little black bag and his polished shoes and his hat, and soon we reached the heads. I stood back and watched him then, as he bent over them. From the rear cockpit an arm was pulled out, white and clean, with a torn sleeve, and a needle was pushed into it. But the head in the front was slumped very low, for we were too late. The rescue crew from the ambulance set to work, crowding on both sides, cutting, pulling, undoing buckles, working tensely, wasting no words. Other men came, country men and rough-looking people from the filling station with their dogs, and the dogs sniffed at the wreck with more than ordinary interest, and nosed around. A pompous fellow arrived and stood up and waved a badge, shouting, "No smoking!" and minutes later I saw him reach in his pocket and light a cigarette. As we stood apart, watching, I slipped my arm through Don's, and felt comfort and thankfulness for his presence. We were strictly onlookers now; we had done our part. We began to look around. What was the thing? Odd-looking bits were scattered everywhere. I could see no propeller, nor any splinters of one, and no engine. Could it have been thrown over the rocks by the impact? A battered book lay at my feet and as I puzzled, I kicked it, and picked it up. "Jet trainer log!" The thing was a jet! And another book lay there in the wreckage, covered with mud and oil: "The Psychology of Women" by Helene Deusch. And all kinds of pieces of metal, radios and compasses, all torn out. Heavy fragments, thrown far up the hill by the shock of the crash. And two helmets, bloody and broken, far from their heads.

Presently a stretcher was brought alongside, and the rescuers lifted him by the shoulders and gradually pulled him out, his legs hanging limp as they trailed over the edge of the wing. "Oh, my legs!" he cried. "Oh! God!" As they laid him down one leg twisted outward and a trickle of fresh blood spread from his groin onto the clean canvas. Someone leaned over and mopped at it with a Kleenex. Fragments of bone stuck out through the torn trouser leg. They fastened the belts on the stretcher and carried him away through the trees. The others went to work on the remains in the front cockpit. Don and I, very tired and sad, turned away and walked slowly up the hill, in among the bits of metal and out onto the track. Then the people began coming. Among the first were three charming girls in high heels and nylons, laughing, looking for the fun. Down there, beyond the bramble patch, we told them. Crowds, in two and threes. Cars all over the road and in the farm-yard. Newsmen with cameras, more crowds, more cars.

They were students in a jet trainer on a cross-country flight, and they had run out of fuel. They had jettisoned the canopy, ready to take to the parachutes, and changed their minds when they saw our large grass field. The pilot underestimated the wind, undershot the runway, stalled and crashed, only a couple of miles from safety. The navigator recovered, after many months in hospital. The book I had found was his, and later, at his request, a diamond engagement ring was recovered from the wreckage.

Many times, in the night, I would wake and listen again to the quietness of the woodland, where the two heads had waited in their broken plane, for help to come. And many times I saw again the dogs sniffing under the cockpits, and saw a white arm raised out of the tangled metal.

n eights

ectangular courses

traffic patterns

Slips

ii) Coordination Maneuvers.

720° power turns

liding spirals

Chande

Lazy eights

lon eights

CHAPTER 8

I have always enjoyed teaching as well as learning; so, when I felt sure that I would not tire of flying, I considered the possibility of teaching others. For this, I needed a Flight Instructor rating. For although a pilot may allow his passenger to take the controls, and may instruct him in the art of flying, no one, other than a licensed instructor, may sign a student's logbook or his permit to solo. An instructor, who may solo a student at his discretion, is thereby committed to responsibility for the behavior of the student, and his knowledge of flying practices which make for safety for himself and others. Most instructors, very rightly, are loathe to sign logbooks and solo students whom they have not trained.

During the early years of my flying, I thought of an instructor as one on a pinnacle of competence and experience far and away beyond my reach. But as my hours in the air accumulated slowly, and as my bounced landings became less frequent, I thought more and more of the possibility of attempting the impossible. I thought of it, but I pushed it out of my mind. Flight instructors are young men, professional fliers who make it their business, and not elderly women who flit around when the weather suits them. Then again I might get what I wanted, for after all, teaching is my work, and I love it. And, if not elegant, I believed myself to be a reasonably safe and careful pilot. I had never met a woman instructor, but I knew that there were some. Oh, how wonderful it would be, to be good enough to teach, and to hold an official Flight Instructor rating!

The first person I spoke to about it was my instructor, George. George, who knew so much and whose advice I trusted, had always done everything he could to encourage me. And he did, once again.

"Yes, go ahead," he said. "No reason why not." But I knew many reasons why not. I was a woman, and not young. I knew what many men would feel about it. An old woman, seeking a Flight Instructor rating! "Making a fool of herself," the young men would say. I could hear them. "Look, her hair is grey. She's too old to fly, anyway!"

So, forget the idea of ever being an instructor, it's impossible. There are things one cannot do, situations one cannot create. But as I flew around the block of an evening I would find myself practicing stalls or lazy eights, and then at night I would lie and dream, and consider my errors and how to improve them. I looked up the regulations. First, one must pass a written exam on the theory of teaching; that should not be difficult. Second, a flight test and oral examination, to be given only by the District Civil Aeronautics Safety Agent himself; maneuvers to be performed . . . at the discretion of the Agent. This, then, was the hurdle. The flight tests for all other certificates and ratings are given by inspectors, of whom there are many. They are usually to be found at large airports, where much teaching is done. And, for each flight test, certain definite maneuvers are specified in the regulations. The discretion of the Agent? He might ask me to do anything, and expect my performance to be perfect.

As I flew around visiting airports in the neighborhood, and talking to people in the repair shops or offices, I would lead the conversation around to the Agent, and I would listen, with very special interest, to what was said about him. What sort of person was he, and what standards did he expect? I got plenty of stories, first-, second- and third-hand, from pilots who had failed their tests. He was said to be fussy. No smoking near an airplane, and he failed a man for such a little thing as lifting his parachute by the risers! And he asked the most detailed questions on the oral exam, and he couldn't fly worth a darn! All this, and more! And I was told, sometimes nicely, and sometimes with rancor, that I would be wasting my time. So, after much hesitation, I went one day to talk to the Agent himself, and I asked him, in so many words, whether he would consider me crazy. I had no wish, I told him, to waste his time, or mine, and I recognized that the idea was an unusual one. He had only to say so, and I would not trouble him again, but if he thought I had a chance, I was ready to work for it.

"Indeed," he said at once, "I do not consider it impossible." And he told me what I should work at. Safety, he said, came first, and elegance, and gentle, graceful handling of the plane was next. No violent turns, no power stalls, no acrobatics. So I should certainly go ahead and work, he told me, and write for an appointment when I felt I was ready for the flight test. He wished me success. I left the office happily, for he, at any rate, did not find anything unreasonable in my desire. And so it was, that fall, that I began to work in earnest.

The weather in winter is built of sudden changes, storms, and cold, clear days. In spring, wind; and in summer the afternoons are cluttered up with thunderheads. But in the fall there are often weeks of good flying weather, quiet, windless days when the sun sets early, and the smoke layers in long trails in the hollows. By good fortune, I had taken my first lessons in the fall. Four years later I worked for my Commercial certificate, and now, this was the time to practice and improve my technique, so that perhaps in the late fall, I would be ready to try for the Flight Instructor's rating. But every few days I told myself: This is not possible. I can never become good enough. Yet everything in me wanted it, as a hungry person wants food. If I could get it before the winter, before the weather broke, before the rush and festivities of Christmas when the college kids come home, and before my heavy teaching in medical school in the spring. . . . Oh! if only!

So, in the cool, settled October days, I set deliberately to work, alone with Willie the Aeronca, with no one to advise or help me. I bought a book with descriptions of the maneuvers, and I installed a small and hateful device in the cockpit in front of me. Nothing but a bubble in a curved tube, a sort of two-dimensional spirit level, but a bubble with wanderlust. A dollar-fifty bubble, guaranteed to shout at you how badly you fly! Skid your tail around with the rudder in a thoughtless moment, and the bubble rushes out to one side, and away. Too much stick, causing a slip, and it moves inward. In a good co-ordinated turn, it stays in the center, and maneuvers are all turns of one sort or another. During my first flights with the bubble, it would disappear completely, so far off center it was, and only after considerable coaxing, and straight and level flight, would it return to its place. Later, I could keep it from wandering, and my flying became smooth. So, each day I would read, and decide which of the many errors described in the book were mine, and go out and try to improve. And the next day, some more. Sometimes I seemed better, sometimes worse, and the more I flew, the more I recognized my own deficiencies, and the more I doubted. Wasn't I wasting my time? Wasn't I attempting the impossible? Anyway, I thought, I'm having fun, but I knew, somehow, that fun was not enough.

Often, on those fine afternoons, a group of young men would gather at the airport, mostly students from the college. We would sit on the steps, hangar-flying. Some of them already had their licenses, others hoped to become pilots. They were very polite, and in their presence I could feel that their language was duly restrained. We talked of their problems, mothers and money. Whatever in the flying game we touched upon, however we talked and laughed together, sooner or later a formula emerged. I got so that I expected it, and waited for it.

"How I wish," one of them would say, "that my mother felt like you do about it!"

Suddenly I am old and different.

"Send her to me," I would say, "and I'll tell her how safe it is." But now there is a great ditch between us. I feel it open up, bottomless and impassible. They must think I'm crazy, but I don't care—or do I? Full of doubts and full of certainties, I start up the Aeronca for a practice flight. Tactfully and politely, they enquire of my progress, and ask when I will be ready to take the flight test. I know they wonder what makes me tick, and so do I. I feel rather desperate. I *must* do this.

So, that fall, I flew figure eights, and more eights. Eights beyond a skater's wildest dreams. Eights every way, horizontal and vertical, along or across a road, steep or shallow, high or low. Eights with one wing tip, and then the other, pivoting around a tree, or other "pylon." Eights formed by the track of the airplane's nose on the horizon, or on the rising harvest moon. Eights in my sleep, eights on the Pole Star itself! For the eight is the pilot's ideal pattern, one which uses all controls, and requires equal and opposite turns, and it can be simple, or elaborated to such a degree of precision that it is almost impossible to attain. So pilots love their eights, and have invented them in astonishing variety.

Very early in the lessons, before the solo, the student is taught to make figure eights over a road or other reference line, not only for the sake of practicing well-co-ordinated turns while his attention is concentrated on the earth below, but also for the recognition of wind drift. The airplane, moving always with the air mass around it, as well as with its own power, is carried away from or toward the landmark, and this must be prevented by judicious variations of the steepness of the turns. All this is, of course, in daily use by pilots during approaches and landings. At first it presents a problem to be solved, but later it becomes automatic. By the time this happens, that sort of eight becomes relatively uninteresting, and of the more advanced kinds there are several, including elaborate ones which are only used for show acrobatics. For the instructor rating, I practiced "on pylon" eights, in which the airplane is related to two landmarks (trees, perhaps), as if it were attached to them, first one and then the other, by a string which is swung around. The pylons are selected on level ground with an open field between them, or nearby, in case of an unexpected power failure and emergency landing. Gradually losing altitude, the pilot approaches one of them from the down-wind side. When very low over the trees, one wing is dipped and a turn is started into the wind. The pylon appears in the center of an area, bounded (for instance) by the two struts under the wing. Instantly, like magic, the positions are reversed and the pylon comes to life. It darts and leaps to escape from the shackles, like a fish on a line, caught and played. It starts ahead, and you dive to catch it; it lags, and you slow your speed, coaxing it to catch up. It tries to slide away under you, and you steepen your bank to hold it in place. It darts off again. So, rushing round and round the two trees, you play a guessing game, so that the controls anticipate the movements of the tree. Sometimes a pylon will get away, and there is no regaining it. Worse than its loss would be an amateurish effort, very dangerous at such a low altitude, to skid the wing into place with the rudder. So you give up, count that turn as lost, and fly away and think upon your sins awhile, and then sneak up again and grab the pylon, if you can. Beside the escape of a pylon, I knew that a turn made down wind, or the choice of a pylon which could not be found after completing the turn around the first one, were errors serious enough to mean outright failure in the flight test. How closely the pylon must be kept in place to pass the test, I had no way of knowing. In a wind, these eights can never be perfect, but sometimes in the dusk, when the bumps are smoothed out, a good pilot will hold the pylon almost exactly in place. So, round and round you go, with eyes for nothing but your reference-point. You fly by feel, by instinct, by your muscle tone and sense of balance, and by the sheer joy of being alive and well and over the tree-tops in a little airplane.

Lazy Eights are quite different, and quite as much

fun. There is no sensation of speed, and no dashing about over the trees, for these eights are performed high in the air. They are not truly eights at all, but a series of slow and graceful turns. In Lazy Eights the wings of my plane are like a lady's wide flowing skirts, and the affair is a gentle dance, a minuet. It starts with a dive, or curtsy, down to the floor, skirts spread wide, and then a slow pull-up and turn; the dancer rises to her full height and the skirt swings out as she moves around to another partner. As the half circle is completed, she bows to the man she is leaving, and without a pause starts her curtsy to the next partner. Down to the floor and up again, turning the other way now, round and back, bow and return to the first partner, who is waiting for her. So, without a break in the continuity of the gentle banks and turns, the nose of the plane makes a symmetrical figure of eight above and below the horizon, crossing at a chosen reference point, the turns planned so that the wing tips, first one and then the other, follow the nose through the same point. A lake which reflects the light, a tuft of smoke, or the tall buildings of a town can be used as a landmark on or near the horizon. No one ever flew a Lazy Eight without constant anticipation and planning, for the pressures on the controls are different for each part of each turn. As the air speed changes, the stick and rudder pressures change, too; and a left turn differs from a right turn, because of the propeller torque. You must bank just enough to bring the nose down through the reference point, unbank just enough to be level as a wing tip follows the nose, and dive just enough to pull up without stalling, to make smooth, even curves above and below the horizon.

Just enough, but not a bit too much, for an error cannot be compensated for later. I never flew a perfect Lazy Eight, and I wonder if one has ever been flown? Always and always there is something which could have been done better.

Although, through the fall days, there were times when I was hopelessly inept, I felt that in general my flying was improving. But it was hard work, and often, if one maneuver went well, another defeated me. If I accomplished recognizable Lazy Eights, in the chandelles, as likely as not, I would overshoot the turn, or pull up too soon and stall. A chandelle, which is a co-ordinated dive, turn and pull-up, I found to be relatively easy. My first ones were performed long ago, when I was a child, in India. My father, an army doctor, kept several elephants, to carry him and his equipment on trips through the country, and one of them, Tommy Dodd, a huge and unreliable creature, was my special favorite. He was consistent, they say, only in that he firmly refused to swim or ford a stream unless his wife, Lucy, went first. So on these expeditions, Lucy went along. Tommy delighted and fascinated me, and I would slip away from my Ayah and go down the garden, and I would tell him, in Hindustani, what I expected of him. His trunk tickled as it wrapped gently around my waist, and I giggled as he lifted me high in the air, leaving my stomach behind me. He would swing me out wide in a great arc and up, and finally deposit me on his head, where I would sit at peace with the world until my father found me, and saw to it that I was removed. We had a fine and mutual understanding, Tommy and I; I didn't know that he had killed a man, and he never failed to do exactly what I told him. I think he liked me, playing there on his forehead, and sometimes he would put me down and I would get him a delicacy, a carrot or a piece of sugar, and up again I would go in another chandelle, to stall out on the broad landing deck between his ears. I remember that he had big hairs in the end of his trunk, and he snuffled, looking for carrots. And I remember that U Barnabas, the Burmese cat, liked to sit on his head, too. I thought of these things sometimes as I flew, and then, once more, I would go to work.

First one way, then the other; dive, bank, full throttle, climb and unbank, so that the half-circle turn, and the bank and the climb are all finished exactly together. And then another. For accuracy, in order not to turn too far, I estimated the one-eighty-degree mark by glances at the transmission line below me, a straight scar through the forest, five miles long. That line was useful, too, in helping me count the turns of a spin. Half, one, one and a half, two! This was something I had not yet mastered. Indeed, it was a long time since I had done any spins at all, and I wondered how I would feel about them. At the time that I soloed and got my Private license, spins were required of all candidates; then a few years later the regulations were changed. Now they are included only in the test for the instructor's rating; not ordinary spins, but accurate, precision ones of an exactly specified number of turns.

Light planes don't like to spin. It must be forced upon them, and they will do it only if they have to. Some, like the Stinson, are specially designed to make it difficult, almost impossible. A spin follows a severe stall, when the air flow over the wing surface breaks loose. On the Stinson, there are slots along the leading edge of the wing, so that it has two separate air currents: the flow over the wing which normally keeps the plane flying, and an ancillary flow, through the slots, which takes over when a stall is imminent. Willie the Aeronca has no such contrivances, and in it a stall, combined with vigorous rudder pressure, will start a spin. But as with all light planes, the controls must be held in position throughout, for it will stop as soon as they are relaxed. It is much easier to get out of a spin than to get into one.

And yet, even though I knew the truth of all this, and though I enjoyed my first spins, I gradually developed an uneasiness about them. There is much tragedy associated with spinning airplanes. And it is true that even now many serious accidents involve spins. The aerodynamics are extremely complicated, and to the pilots of the early years the spin was a mystery, and it was the end. No one had ever recovered from one, for, with the elevators already raised to their limit by the stick, which was fully back, how could the nose of the plane ever be pulled up and out of its desperate earth-bound plunge? The story is still told of a brave man, that he preferred, if he had to hit, to hit hard. So he pushed the stick forward, and became the first man ever to recover from a spin! Was he brave enough, I wondered, to repeat the experiment?

Why then do spin accidents still happen? I think it is because there are many ways to stall a plane, and a spin can start out of any of them, with a different feeling to it.

Sometimes there is ample warning, and sometimes almost none. Perhaps it is like this. A pilot makes a steep turn, in the pattern low down for a landing, or over his girl-friend's home. His girl sees him and waves, and he leans out. His bank steepens. He knows that the wing is too low, and he tries to hoist it with the stick, which he pulls into the upper, back, corner. Tense, he pushes on the low rudder. The wing doesn't respond, for he is near a power-on stall. Hold on hard, he thinks; it's going out of control! He jitters on the rudders, or a gust hits him, and the plane stalls suddenly in a steep skidding turn. In a flicker of an eye he is in a spin (a power spin, too) without altitude to recover, even if he knew what had happened. Different, indeed, from the deliberate spin, when after the approach to a power-off stall there are several seconds of hesitance, while the plane's nose rises, and slowly it lurches forward and down, before it starts to rotate.

So a pilot, before he flies safely, must learn a very difficult lesson, one which is contrary to all his natural instincts. A headlong descent toward the ground? Pulling back won't help you! You must let go of the stick, so that it moves forward. A wing that won't come up? Let go! The airplane can look after itself better, now, than you can do! Turn it loose! Then, and only then, you may guide it gently where you want it to go.

After a busy, tiring day, one choked with petty irritations, I found that I had an hour to spare. I was too tired, I decided, to do any air work; I would allow myself the luxury of wandering, and enjoy myself. When I reached the airport, I was not sorry to find it deserted, and the wind sock limp under a quiet, overcast sky. I pushed Willie out onto the apron and checked it for gas and oil, slowly and deliberately savoring the very special flavor that airplanes have for me. I chocked the wheels and pulled the propeller. As I taxied out to the end of the runway and waited there for the engine to warm, my tiredness seemed to drop away from me, and my sense of anticipation increased. I took off, and climbed.

The air was like silk, and the horizon clear. At three thousand feet, I was still far below the mottled overcast. I decided to do some spins. I was glad to find that I had not even the faintest apprehension as I made the preliminary clearing turns, looking carefully all around me, and pulled out the carbureter heat. An ordinary power-off stall till it mushes, and then with the stick hard back, give it full rudder, whichever way you want to spin. Oh, what a poor attempt! A messy, sloppy spiral! So I got out of it, and started afresh, and spiraled again. And one can pick up too much air speed that way. So I went back to straight and level flight, and sat a while to consider my errors. I had lost the touch of a clean spin entry. Something was wrong with my technique, and Willie wouldn't spin. Vexed at myself, I decided to try something I had never done before, something the book says, use a quick blast of throttle to give the rudder some slipstream to work on, to start the rotation just as it stalls.

Long ago, as a child of ten, my birthday gift from my father was a Shetland pony, no bigger than a big dog. I remember my first sight of him, with his small, elegant feet beneath long dark hair, as he picked his way neatly through the open door of his wooden traveling crate. He was fat and shaggy, and as I walked toward him to make friends, he bit. A mouthful of coat was all he got, but our dislike for each other was instant and mutual, and lasted through the several years of his residence in our stable. His favorite trick, when I wanted to saddle him, was to inflate himself while I pulled on the girths to tighten them. I would wait, and pretend indifference, and he would do the same, holding his breath. Finally, I would mount, and with a great sigh his bulging sides would collapse, the saddle would slip around under his belly, and I would be dislodged. Then he would slowly turn his head and gaze at me, and there was no humor in his eye. So I learned to ride him bareback, with my knees tight in the grooves behind his shoulders, and a willow switch in my hand. When he balked, I would use it, and hard. Down would go his head, and up and out would go his heels, and there was nothing but empty air between me and the earth. Somehow, most of the time, I would hold on.

Forty years between the sting of a switch on a pony's rump and the blast of a throttle to spin an airplane, no time at all. Down went Willie's nose and up went his tail, spinning this time. While the great saucer of the fields revolved and I hung in space above it, I started to laugh. Then, let go the rudder pedal, snap; and let the stick go forward, and the spin stopped with a quiver. The road under me stayed in place, and gently, without hurry, I pulled back on the stick until the world was in order again.

No time at all, after all those years, and I was sitting alone in an airplane, two thousand feet up, laughing and happy. Laughing so that my knees shook against the stick, knees which forty years ago had crushed the fur of a mean little pony.

My next problem, now that I could make Willie spin, was to learn to orient myself. I had to find out how to count the turns I was doing, and how to stop the spin far enough ahead so that I would not overshoot. At first, I would get hopelessly lost. As the plane rotated, the whirling movement made me lose track of the earth, even though a road, or the transmission line, lay below me. I would stop the spin, and see which way I was heading, and wonder how many turns I had taken to get there. How many in *that* one? How could I tell? Then suddenly, the situation reversed itself, and I found that now it was not I, but the earth, that was revolving. Now, I was poised, nose down, in the middle of a landscape which moved without hurry, as if pivoted beneath the nose of the plane. And now it was easy to count the turns. I could look ahead and see the power line as it came around and passed at each half turn. Half, one, one and a half, two!

In all those weeks that I worked, practicing maneuvers, I had no help from anyone; I worked alone. I knew, from the book, how each maneuver should be done, and I knew the unforgivable sins, the errors that meant certain failure. But in one respect I was helpless, for I did not know what degree of perfection could be acquired. I had no basis for comparison. Most of the time, now, my plane's bubble indicator looked out from the center of its prison window, and now, almost every time, I could do a spin of one or two complete turns. Nowadays, too, once I had a pylon securely hooked, even though it struggled and danced, it rarely succeeded in breaking loose. I was, without doubt, a much better and smoother pilot than I used to be, and it was getting near to winter. I felt that the time had come to take the test. I had done as much as I could. It was now or never. So, deliberately ignoring the possibility that I was making myself more than slightly ridiculous, I wrote to the Safety Agent for an appointment for a flight test.

About two weeks later, on a raw and windy November day, I drove out to the airport to find the official car already in the parking place. The Agent looked me over with a stern and businesslike aspect as we walked to the hangar, and he watched my every movement as I reached into the box where my borrowed parachute was kept, and pulled it out and carried it to the plane. Whatever you do, don't hold it by the risers, I remembered; they say he'll fail you for that. How remote and impersonal he seemed. Two people we were, two people with only one bridge between our separate worlds. If I failed this test, it wouldn't really matter. I could go on flying anyway.

As we walked among the planes sitting there in the gloom of the hangar, bending our heads under the wings and propellers, he started asking questions: weather, theory of flight, engines; why I wanted permission to teach; and silly, idle questions such as a student might ask, intricately mixed with technical ones, many of which I could not answer.

"You seem to know plenty about it," he said. "Now we will go. People say," he continued, to my surprise, "that I can't fly, and they are right! I don't work with these small planes, and one gets out of practice. But don't make any mistake," he said with emphasis, "I know what good flying is!" With that, he stepped into the harness of his parachute, and I did the same, watching him, trying to follow his method, hoping that mine was the same type as his, and fitted on the same way. I had only tried the thing once or twice, a great clumsy pack with complicated harness, to be used, according to the regulations, during any flight involving acrobatics. Would I ever, I wondered, really be in need of a chute? It seemed unlikely! Or would I ever have the courage to make a deliberate, planned jump? Then the Agent climbed into the front seat of the Aeronca, the student's seat. I saw him take out his notebook and pencil, and fasten his seatbelt. Now, I thought, this is the time when the little beast will be ornery and refuse to start. I climbed in behind, while the attendant stood at the propeller, waiting for instructions. How wide those shoulders seemed, blocking me from the instrument panel. Often, long ago when I was a student, George would tell me to relax, and I remember how once he yelled at me while we were spinning.

"What did you shout at me for?" I asked him later.

"You were tense," he answered. "I knew by your shoulders. I was just telling you to relax!"

Perhaps it was better, after all, to have him there, in front and not behind me, even if it were difficult to see the instruments. I could see the important ones, which are installed at the extreme sides of the panel, and I could see the others if I raised myself and peeked. I felt strange, with the chute behind me. I should have worn it more often, for it

changes one's position relative to the airplane, but one is
conspicuous around an airport wearing one of the things;
they think you are trying to look like a stunt pilot.

"Off?" cried the attendant. "Off!" I echoed. "Contact!" "Contact!" and the Aeronca started at the first pull.
Oh, good, I thought, a lucky omen. Oh, but how foolish, to
look for signs and portents, like the ancients watching the
birds. We, who can build our own birds! How I would
have liked to know what he was thinking, there in front
of me, more remote than ever. He turned around.

"Fly the pattern," he said. "Three times round the
field." This wind, I thought; it's picking up. Now for it!
Don't forget any detail. Attention to little things counts a
lot. Taxi down wind with the stick forward, so that the
elevators are tucked in, to prevent the wind from getting
under the tail. And the controls work in reverse, naturally,
when the wind is from the rear. Wing down into the
wind as you turn. Women have an advantage here, they
have learned to handle big hats; it's the same problem,
don't ever let the wind get underneath. Use the throttle if
there is any trouble, if she starts out of control. Check the
engine, it sounds fine. As we raced along the runway the
butterflies in my stomach settled down, almost before we
left the ground. Up we went, lifted by the wind. I forgot
the Agent. I was at home and happy now, doing my best
at a job I loved, working hard to control the plane, to
make it fly where I wanted it to go. I fought the wind with
everything in me, and I fought it to a perfect three-point
landing. Another take-off, and as we came around the field,
I felt the Agent stirring in his seat, and he reached out

with his hand, and very deliberately covered the dial of the air-speed indicator! Now what? How could I judge my air speed now? Ground speed, in that gale, would fool you. Up wind, we seemed almost to stand still, and down wind the trees and houses raced past me in a hurry; I must be careful not to stall out, thinking I have too much speed. I must concentrate, use all my senses, fly by feel, do my best anyway. I knew where the dangers lay. It would be easy, any day but this! I decided to make a wheel landing this time, for I could come in fast for that. They are good for just such winds, to keep plenty of control. We stuck as if glued to the sod, and the Agent removed his hand. The third time round we used another runway, cross wind, and I fought the wind again, using different weapons, and again we were down. So far, I thought, this doesn't seem too bad. But I wished I could see the Agent's expression, as he turned halfway round to give me some instructions, and made some marks in his notebook.

Now we flew to some open fields, away to the west, for pylon eights. As I indicated the direction of the wind, I chose a tree in the middle of an open field, and turned into the wind around it; that was one pylon. Turning on the down-wind side to look for another one, I saw, a mile away, a junction of five roads, and I saw on one of them a place where the dark surface changed sharply to light. Now on blue and white days, when clouds sail in fleets, these changes are familiar, where shade and sunshine meet. Perhaps several will chase each other, very fast, along the roads and over the hedges. But today there was no sun, and this one was not moving. Asphalt and concrete, probably a county boundary line. I could use it as a second pylon, and I swung the little plane into a co-ordinated turn around it. Round we went until we saw my tree again, level up, gauge the wind velocity to counteract drift, and fly to it; round again, a neat eight that time. Now for the line dividing dark and light, my other pylon; I looked along the highway. I looked again, desperately now, and it had gone! I couldn't find it! It must have been a tiny patch of sun, a break through, a sucker hole, they call them! The pylon was lost, the unpardonable sin committed! And then far to the right, down wind, I saw it. I had picked the wrong road, another of the five that met there below me, and there I was, on the wrong side of the pylon, unable to make a turn into the wind around it. The second unforgivable sin! My heart sank and my spirits collapsed as I studied the shoulders in front of me. What did we do now? I had wasted my chance, and all those weeks of work. I couldn't possibly pass the test, after that. Yet, if the rest was exceptionally good, could he? I had chosen a fossil shadow. Oh, what a fool I had been! A shadow for a pylon! Was that the way I flew? But it wasn't, it was real, and I had been stupid enough to lose it. Would he tell me to fly back home in disgrace? He turned half round.

"Climb to two thousand, and do a chandelle," he said. But the heart had gone out of my flying and the chandelle was uneven. "Spin it," he said, and as we turned toward home I kicked at the rudders and held the stick full back. Then my foot slipped, and I felt the spin tighten up, and the Agent moved in his seat as if to take the controls. I let go of the rudders and pushed on the stick, and with a jerk the spinning stopped. A bad spin and a poor recovery, and I did a poor landing, too. Deeply discouraged, I helped push the plane into the hangar, and turned to the Agent to learn my fate. After such a demonstration, would he ever allow me to try again?

"Of course I cannot pass you," he said, and the words stung me as I heard them, for even then I had hoped for the impossible.

"Yes, of course I know," I said. "But would you count me a reasonably safe pilot?" and instantly I could have kicked myself, to ask such a thing.

"Absolutely safe," he said. "I'd let my children ride with you."

"Will I be troubling you, if I try again?"

"I hope you will," he said as he went off.

A few days later I received in the mail a list of my sins, and it was even worse than I had thought. I had failed everything, except the oral exam and the three landings. I considered the matter in every detail, and I flew the flight again and again. I heard again the words of the Agent, and his tone as he spoke of his children. He would let them fly with me. I felt suddenly warm toward him, and I felt better. I had a good idea, now, of what was wanted. Yes, I would try again.

For a time, I could not bring myself to practice. And yet I knew I could try once more; only once. Not because of any official ruling, either, but because of the unwritten laws that govern the conduct of middle-aged women. For a week of fine and quiet days I stayed at home in the afternoons, digging in my garden, thinking of the airplanes, and running out from under the trees at the sound of an engine. Where was it? Who was it? What did the world look like from up there today? Then, one windy, restless afternoon, I took my car and went to the airport. Once more, Willie and I fought the wind. Wham! It hit us on the final approach. Wham! Again. And we were high over the hangar. Wham! The bottom fell out below us, and we were down, and then started to fly again. Sit down, I told him, sit and stay down! And we sat. Joyfully, the next day and the next I was out again, at work, harder than ever. The same maneuvers, and a couple I had not practiced; more spins, eights and chandelles. Then, once more, the formal letter from the Agent, in answer to mine. This time he would meet me at Burlingford airport, where the airliners land; he set a date, a week ahead. But in the middle of the week the rains began, December, winter rains, and I knew that my chances for a fine flying day were very slim.

On the afternoon before the appointment I stood in the hangar, behind the closed doors, in drenching rain. I had already talked with the Weather Bureau. A cold front was on the way, which, if it kept up its present speed, should pass us in the early morning, followed by the usual "clearing, windy and colder" weather. It must be over the Alleghenies now, I thought, and that is where the guess-work starts. Sometimes a front will lose forward speed, becoming sluggish as it climbs over the great rock wall which lies between it and the sea. Or, it will have push enough to reach the mountain crests, and fall over itself, hurrying down the slope and across the plain, as fast, or faster, than before. A few hours, either way, could make all the difference to my chances. Ten o'clock, the Agent had written, and if it wasn't flying weather, of course we could plan another day, but for me, it seemed as if it had to be tomorrow. Lately, it had occupied such a large part of my time, and I had planned and worked for so long! Oh, give me this chance, I begged; give me clear skies and a gentle wind! In the dim light I watched the gale pushing the rain water in little waves into the hangar, up from under the big metal sliding doors, farther and farther like the flow of the tide, until the waves lapped against the wooden chocks, and even touched the Aeronca's wheels. I sat in the gloomy cockpit, planning, maneuvering, while the gusts rattled the tin roof. The cards seemed stacked against me. Even if the rain stopped, the field would be deep in water, and I might not be able to get off. And in such moisture-soaked air, engines get wet, and Willie might not start. So ran my sad thoughts as I opened the doors and looked out. A gust came round the corner and flattened the tall grasses that grew there, and wisps of cloud came down over the hill, obscuring the ends of the runways. I squeezed out, shut the door behind me, and my raincoat ballooned as I ran through the mud to my car.

In the morning the sun shone. I woke sharply, and lay for a moment uncertain of what it was that made the day so important. Then my mind caught hold, and my stomach turned over. By tonight I would know; either I would be a flight instructor, or I would never become one. What a stupid way to look at it! Out of the window I could see the sun touching the tops of the pine trees, shining in the clean, wet needles. I told myself: Don't act like a teen-ager. The worst possible thing is to get tense and jittery. Be calm, relaxed and indifferent. Do your best anyway, and don't think about the situation.

Out at the airport, it was hard to believe the change from the grey world of yesterday to the new, brightly washed one that I found there. Willie started at the first pull. A little spray of water splashed away from the wheels as I taxied out, and as I shoved the throttle forward for take-off, the spray became a shower, dousing the under-surface of the wings. My speed increased, then slowed as we hit a puddle. I tried the stick; no lift yet, no flying speed. Faster again, then slow. Would we get off? Then came a little burst of speed, and the stick came back as we broke from the wet ground. I took up the course for Bur-lingford, and glanced at my watch. Just after nine o'clock. I was airborne!

A half hour later I landed, chocked the Aeronca and went into the office. I waited. Ten fifteen, and no Agent, and then he telephoned. He was sorry to be delayed, could I wait till eleven? Back and forth I walked, waiting. Two young men came in; an instructor and his student. He signed the student's logbook and turned to me.

"Waiting for the Agent?" he asked me. "Private?"

"No," I said briefly, remote and unhappy.

"Commercial?" he persisted.

"No. Flight Instructor's rating!" And he looked so astonished that in spite of myself I laughed out loud! He laughed, too, a nice easy laugh, and he made me welcome. Together we sat by the stove with a pot of hot coffee, and while I tried to control my shivers he told me his flying history, and asked about mine. At eleven, the Agent called again; it would be at least twelve thirty before he could make it. The minutes dragged as we talked, and, at intervals, my stomach hit bottom. But at last it ended, and he came in, businesslike but friendly.

Then we flew. It was all simple. Cross-wind take-off, straight as a die. The horizon clear as crystal. Over some fields to the northeast, we turned and wound and unwound ourselves. What came over Willie that day, I shall never know, but I know that I was one with him. I rode him like Pegasus; together we planned and banked and turned. After a chandelle, the Agent looked back and made a sign of approval, but I was too busy to take much notice. I flew, and flew. I never, ever before, flew like that, so utterly happy, so completely at ease with the plane, so surely guiding it through the required patterns. Pylons, chandelles and all, with never a question or a demand for a repeat, we went through the paces. We started back. Oh! I had flown well, I had done the best that was in me, better than I had believed possible, but how could I tell whether it was good enough? I longed to lean forward and say to the shoulders, "I don't know whether I've been good enough, but however you decide, I want you to know that I've done my best, and that I've had fun. Oh! what fun!"

We landed, and taxied in silence up the long, long runway to the ramp. My heart sank as I cut the engine and we got out. It wasn't good enough, then. Well, now for it. It wasn't, I knew it wasn't.

"A *much* better flight than last time," said the Agent.
"Yes, I know, but it wasn't good enough, was it?"
"Congratulations!" He shook my hand.
"Thank you," I gasped. "You deserved it!" he said.
"You did well."

In the office, he typed me a temporary certificate, and signed my logbook.

Back to Willie, in a daze. The green light from the tower cleared me for take-off, and I rose again into a glorious sky. Passing the tower, level with it, I saw the little figures in the control room. What a pylon the tower would make! How those fellows would run! My fingers itched to make a sudden turn toward it and fly round it, round and round for sheer joy. I could barely hold Willie back! I thought of the Agent, watching perhaps. Certainly they would telephone him, and my new rating would be canceled! Instructor for an hour . . . no . . . less than half an hour, she must be crazy, they'd say; she buzzed the tower! I pictured the traffic controller at the hearing. "It turned sharply and came right at us. We dived under the table. . . . How could I see the identification? I tell you I was under the table! It flew several times round, wing tips almost touching the glass, before it went off!" "Yes, I know, but I couldn't help it," I'd say. "You see Willlie took charge that day. *He* flew the maneuvers, *he* buzzed the tower, not I." I tore myself away and headed for home. I climbed to three thousand feet, and leveled off, and let go of everything. I started to sing. I shouted, I sang and I yelled. I whispered to Willie how I loved him, darling Willie, and I sang some more. The impossible had come to pass, the unbelievable was true! Back home, high over the airport, I put Willie into three loops, one after the other, and then I went spinning down.

"Whatever in the world got into you?" said Poppa from the middle of a group of students. "Do you think that spring has come?"

He didn't know about the bit of paper in my wallet, and I joked and laughed, but I didn't tell him. He would find out, presently.

CHAPTER 9

O_n a cold January evening, Frederick spoke of a trip to Los Angeles in September, to attend a conference.

"Why don't we fly the Stinson?" he said.

I looked up from the book on my knee, as we sat one on each side of the blazing fire. The shadows of the flames played up and down on his face, hiding his expression.

"Do you mean it?" I asked. "Do you think we could?"

Could we fly until the Pacific was ahead of us and we could go no farther? No, I thought, it isn't possible. We don't have enough experience to plunge into such an undertaking. I had heard talk of air currents that create fierce turbulence among the Rockies, fierce enough to trap a small airplane in a narrow pass. And of the thunder among the peaks. And of the fog banks along the coast, that cover the airports with no warning, and of the Los Angeles smog. It is different flying, I had heard it said, and it's all right if you know how to do it! But already the dichotomy of the flying game was tearing at my guts, and the book I had been reading was forgotten. To fly west and more west, out over lands which were new and ever changing with the passing hours. To see salt flats, grain elevators, oil wells, canyons, all new shapes and colors. To cross the Mississippi and the Rio Grande and the Colorado so that they became real to me, and I could take home the essence of each one of them in my mind, caught there for always. And I thought not only of the trip and all that it might mean, but also of the return; the final landing back at the Hill, and the first evening at home again. How, waking perhaps in the quiet nights, I would select carefully, from my great store, whichever of all the different episodes appealed to my taste at the moment. There would be bland and delicate flavors, and perhaps some strong ones, highly seasoned, and gay, humorous ones, all of them delicious in retrospect, tasted and retasted in the night from my ground floor bedroom!

To Frederick, that evening, I said, "That *would* be fun!"

I had always wanted to see the West. But still I hesitated, loading myself down with insecurities. Did I really want to take off, destination California? I attempted the impossible, to balance the unknown on already-weighted scales. Then, unexpectedly it seemed to me, my doubts and worries dropped away. Other people have done this, I said to myself, ordinary people like us, not adventurers, and so can we. The days before take-off would be the worst for me, I knew. The Rockies would swell until they were insurmountable, and there would be nothing to navigate by, no tracks in the endless desert sand. Yet I knew how much, how very much, I wanted to go.

I looked at Frederick and puzzled, as I have done many times during our life together. Did he want to go, without any reservations or inner turmoil? He would never say how he felt. Did he find things so easy? If so, he was lucky. No—he wasn't lucky, for in that way he missed the very circumstances which made the delight of accomplishment. The spice would go out of it, if it were all simple.

Gradually, we planned not to plan. The West was new to both of us. We would go, or stay, where we liked. We owed ourselves a vacation, for it was years since we had been away together, for a real holiday. We would be at ease and unhurried, and fly only in good weather.

I wrote to the Airplane Owners and Pilots Association for expert advice. We had to consider the best route for our Stinson, the location of airports at which we could refuel, and the heights of the mountains, for we carry no oxygen. I ordered aerial navigation charts, those directly on our way, and extra ones, both north and south of our course, in case we needed them. Presently they came in the mail, enough to fill a suitcase, looking very important. That evening I spread them out in order, like a carpet on the living-room floor, and at once I got myself into trouble. The things reached across the room and more! How could we do it? On hands and knees I crawled about over them, noting the positions of the cities on our course, while I measured, calculating speed and time. Chart after chart lay before me, a never-ending procession. The first ones on the way were thickly speckled with towns, laced together by irregular networks of roads and railways. Later, there were very few, and many areas were completely bare. Instead of pale green, a light brown covered the charts as the elevation of the land increased. Could the Coast and Geodetic Survey have made a mistake, and was this a chart of the moon? I wondered. I studied them closely, to suck from them every precious detail, but only so much would they yield, and so much was missing. I tried to see the shapes of the mountains and the flat, high plateaus, the color and smell of the air, the feeling of the dawns and twilights. I saw, instead, the thin line of the road and railroad, not running directly east and west, as we would travel, but wandering, apparently aimlessly, sometimes south, sometimes north, of our course; a few small towns; here and there water holes in the desert, miles apart, and lava beds.

We decided to buy, for the Stinson, a marvelous radio and navigating device, a VHF (very high frequency) transmission and reception radio, equipped with a needle which, picking up messages from the omniranges, indicates to the pilot his bearing from the omni station. Center the needle, keep it centered, and it will lead you home. And scattered over the land, almost anywhere you want to go, even across the desert, such omni stations are in action, sending out their signals day and night. They are arranged so that one can fly from one to the next, all the way from New York to Los Angeles. We had troubles, though, with our new machine. At first I thought it was cockpit trouble, but after several push-button sessions with it, we seemed to be operating it correctly. For a while it worked alternately, Mondays but not on Sundays, a forty-hour week, we thought. We asked other pilots who were experienced with such things. "You have to get the bugs out of it, and get to know it," they told us, "and then you'll never want to be without it." "But," added the wise ones, "you may trust it, but not too much. Don't ever forget to navigate by the ground, as well." Finally, when we flew to New York to visit the parents before our trip, I was satisfied with the way it worked.

At Westchester County airport, the day before our take-off, we checked the Stinson in great detail. We put water in the battery and air in the tires, the oil and gas tanks were filled, and the engine and radio seemed in order. We packed the baggage compartment with some tools, and a few spare parts, and some extra oil of the brand we use. Feeling mildly foolish, I added a small, sharp hatchet, and a container for water, just in case. Emergencies do happen!

At the family home, I detected a troubled atmosphere, especially at the dinner party our parents had planned for our last evening. I think they felt the way I did before I learned to fly, and so I was sorry for them. It was useless to tell them how safe our venture would be, how much safer than driving a car. The Stinson, to them, was as safe as a raft in mid-Pacific, or a flying carpet. And too, although this was my secret, mine alone, and although I spoke of our trip with an air of confidence, my insides *were* a trifle curled up, and my throat knotty. Alone among us, Frederick, I thought, has no such feelings.

The next morning the whole family came to see us take off. The two suitcases went into the baggage compartment, and a brief case loaded with charts, pencils, rulers, protractors, notebooks, lists of Weather Bureau telephone numbers (the special aviation ones), Flight Information Manual, and the latest edition of the Airman's Guide, came into the cabin with me. It was our most valuable possession, and it stayed by my side for the next five weeks, day and night, like a diplomatic pouch. Formalities, goodbyes . . . a bit strained, but not so difficult as I expected. Frederick started the engine.

I climbed in and turned the new omni onto the tower. We heard them chattering busily, but they did not answer when we called them. Try again. Cuss the radio, wretched thing, it's out again! Reception fine, transmission dead. The parents are waving to us, Goodbye, goodbye. Take off for California (Yes, that's what we are doing!) with the radio out? We moved slowly out and turned, and the tower, at last, cleared us. Then we were off, wiggling our wings to the little group of relatives on the grass, like ants now, their arms like waving antennae. First stop, Johnstown, Pa. When we leveled off, on course, I began to fiddle with the omni, and I worked at it for quite a while. Then I turned to Frederick.

"I'm sorry," I said, shamefaced. "That was my fault. Button trouble! I won't make that mistake again." We had been broadcasting to an omnirange which wasn't there, instead of the tower!

We flew most of that day, until we were almost at Columbus. At first it was sunny, but presently we came to a filthy mess of smog, thick in the valley of the Ohio River. We landed in rain, but the next morning was clear, and we crossed the Mississippi at St. Louis before time for lunch. Both of us, I think, looked for a change here, although we did not know what, and we found it at the next landing, for Springfield, Mo. is a clean and lovely place, and the wind that blew across the airport was sharp and sweet. Tulsa was two hours away, so we could get there before dark; we would make eight hundred and fifty miles, I figured, in six and three quarter hours. I was getting tired now, and looked forward to the last landing of the day, and a quiet meal, and early to bed. We must be nearing Tulsa now. The dusk was settling on us as we passed, exactly on course, over a large reservoir with easy, unmistakable check-points. Ten more miles or so. I tuned the radio to the tower of the huge airport, and listened. There were no breaks in the stream of talk that issued from the man in the tower. It was not a conversation; it was a monologue; eddies whirled, ripples parted and met again, but the main flood of his words went on and on. He spoke to airliners, jets; there must be traffic everywhere. *Where* was he? So near and clear, out of somewhere into everywhere, he chattered, but *where*? I strained my eyes into the thickening evening, and peered all round us. We couldn't be far off course. My mind went back to the water, my last check-point. Too far south? Or north? At last we found the air-port. And at last, somehow, Frederick caught our identification in the chattering stream, and held on. "Cleared to land," said the tower. "Expedite your taxiing, I have three jets behind you!" We scurried off the runway and onto the taxi strip, and moved along, past a long row of hangars. At last we found a place for the Stinson. I was tired and hungry. While Frederick unpacked the suitcases, I went into the office, past three men sitting at a table.

"May I use the phone?" I asked. "Which hotel do you recommend?"

Slowly the men looked at me, and I looked at them, puzzled. Was this so unusual a request, in Oklahoma?

"You see, M'm, there's not a room to be had in town. The Shriners are here!"

"*You* telephone," said Frederick when I told him. "Put on a show. Stranded woman and all that. We must find something!" But it was no show I put on, it was the real thing. The hotel manager, after a long pause, found us a room on the top floor, and apologized for it. He didn't have to! It was not air-conditioned, he said, he was sorry it was the best he could do. The hotel lobby was a solid sea of Shriners; we finally took the freight elevator to the top floor, and all night long we tried to sleep, to the astonishing catcalls, hoots, sirens and other noises of the Tulsa night.

I quote from my notes, written the next evening:

"Lazy navigator takes Turner Turnpike, into Okla-homa City, Tulakes Airport, nice place. Oil derricks, my first, are decorative from above. The lakes seem to have no depth, just surface ponds. At take-off I got disoriented and then located Yukon, a tiny place with the first grain elevator. We crossed the Canadian River, a wide sweep of pale yellow sand, washed out miles wide from recent floods, water now only a tiny trickle. Fields red, river sand stood out white for ever so far. Followed the highway (why not?) through wide-open country, strange square fields, many with dark green, mossy-looking areas, round like mold, on a pale green background. Low bushes? Fields red and yellow, green and purple. Grain elevators here and there along the road, lonely among the colors. More green, dark moss. North Fork Red River, another ribbon of washed-out sand. Land gradually, invisibly, rising. I would have guessed sea level, but for the color of the chart. Amarillo Airport is 3,500 feet! Land incredibly flat. Brilliant colors in patchwork, and a train, like a worm creeping over the vast plain. Bright, white grain elevators far away. Many little ponds without any banks to hold them in place. They seemed ready to run around, like quicksilver on a tabletop. Many had grass or reeds growing right in the middle of them; maybe the grass anchored them in place, or maybe they moved, during the night. More rain than usual this year, they say. We landed in a steady, howling wind, tied down, and ate. Then we called Albuquerque for reservations and found, as we expected, that the Shriners were there first. There was no rooms to be had in town, even the dormitories of the university were full of Shriners. We must wait. Tomorrow, perhaps, we can go as far as Tucumcari."

Tucumcari . . . the first desert airport, the last refuge before the great barrier of mountains; the western end of the flat plains, the lands of oil, wheat and cattle, and the eastern edge of the uninhabited wilderness of sand and rock. The meeting place of two worlds.

We got a ride into town, found a pleasant Spanish hotel near the railroad station, and when the sun was low we went out for a walk. The wind was strong against us and supported us as we leaned forward. We walked a long way and scrambled up a hill beyond the town, and there in front of us was Tucumcari Mountain, five miles away, so near we could almost touch it. Now, from the ground, we could see the flat top and the steep sides, and even the grain of the bright red rock. It must have been, long ago, part of the immense tableland that lay to the south. We could see the edge, curving away until it faded into the far distance. Strange cactus shapes and stiff, dry bushes were all around us. We stayed there a long time. This was a delicious new world, and as we stood there together the rock of the mountain turned incandescent and then bloody in the setting sun. The sweet wind from the mesas was like wine, bringing a fine, exciting bouquet to my awakened senses; a reviving wind, that blew the dust out of me. The bushes rustled and squeaked. As we turned home, the evening became night, and the desert stars popped out above us.

The time to fly the mountains, they told us, is very early in the morning. Start as soon as you can see to take off. Fog does not keep you waiting here, the way it does back in the Alleghenies, where it clutters up the valleys until the sun burns it off. And the morning air is smooth, before the rising currents make turbulence, and the cumulus clouds turn into dangerous thunderheads. The range of mountains between us and Albuquerque was as high as any we would cross. Don't follow the road through the pass, but get enough altitude to clear the saddlebacks and fly straight over them. Tomorrow promised to be a good flying day.

We were early at the airport, but the sky to the west was black and heavy, although the east was clear. You can't tell much by that, I thought; light like this is very deceptive. It was cold. The offices, hangars and coffee shop were tight shut. Only the Weather Bureau was awake, and we went along the raised boardwalk over the sand, shivering. As we opened the screen door of the brightly lighted hut a crowd of large lace-winged flies rose up, and settled again as the door slammed behind us. Several people were there, and I recognized the sleek pilot who had landed just behind us yesterday, and his companion, worried and frowning. We heard them, discussing sky conditions and terminal forecasts for the El Paso area, and at Roswell, on the way. The low clouds were reported on the tops of the Sacramento Mountains, and there was an upper layer at eighteen hundred. Improvement was not expected. The sleek man made no comment. He turned on his heel and went out, followed by his friend.

Another couple were there, a man and his young wife, heading east. For them the forecast was good, and they went off. "Happy landings!" called the woman as she waved to me. "Albuquerque?" said the weatherman.

"Otto. The last report from Otto. The peaks are hidden. Clouds broken, at twenty-five hundred." I knew about Otto, the omnirange station east of the pass. We would fly over Otto, a tiny, round, busy, white building, filled with radio equipment. Inside, an attendant kept the omnirange in working order, reported the weather conditions, checked and recorded pilots' Flight Plans, and answered the inquiries of aircraft within the range. "There's another report due in thirty minutes." "Thank you. We'll wait," Frederick said. We turned away, and as we opened the door a plane rushed low over us; the sleek pilot had taken off to find El Paso. "Those," said the weatherman with a flick of his head, "are the ones who get into trouble!"

The airport woke as the sun rose, and the shadows shortened. We moved our chairs into the shade. We watched the rabbits that played hide-and-seek under the broken boardwalk, their heads popping up through the holes in unexpected places, their stiff pointed ears exquisitely blended with the background color. We fed them bread and lettuce scraps from yesterday's sandwiches, and they hopped nearer as they became bolder. The cloud bank was breaking, surely. The report from Otto was four thousand five hundred scattered, so we left.

Climb, nose up, climb some more! Up and up, turning this way and that to avoid the fluffy white clouds. We were in a whole fleet of them; in the corridors among them. They came sailing past us, inquisitive and stately, peeking at us in the cabin. One by one they sidled away behind us, turning as if to look at us as they went. Then we were above them, and as we passed over one I saw, in perfect tiny replica, our Stinson surrounded by a circle of rainbow, on the surface of the cloud. Otto was somewhere down there, and now the mountain wall stretched across our track; sometimes we caught a glimpse of the valley beyond. Unbelievable masses of rock, huge, bare and dead. The altimeter read eleven thousand feet as we crossed the summit, and Albuquerque was clear as crystal below.

Albuquerque to Los Angeles, in one day. A total of twenty-four hours from New York. The last day was six and a half hours, about eight hundred and thirty miles. By road it must be much longer. Who would believe that the lava beds still look as if they had flowed there only a few years ago? The pattern, with great scallops at the edges, still lies there black and scabby, trimmed with a few trees. We made three landings on our way: Winslow first, an unfriendly airport in barren sand. Once in a while, a ripple stirred in the still air, and gradually the movement increased. Then, the air became bumpy. Prescott was a green oasis, with flowers and antelope, doughnuts and coffee. There were woods and a lake, and far out in the forest was a thin wisp of smoke . . . a campfire, surely? Then we were over a rainbow-colored canyon, and the Mohave Desert, where the color went out of the land and it became grey and lifeless. More grey rock, and more. Always rock, ahead and around us. We overflew Needles. The Stinson quivered and pitched now. It was level only for an instant, on its way out of one lurch into the next. Once it lay on its side as if it would turn over, and Frederick pulled the wheel to help it back. The peaks of the Granite Mountains (what a name!) were below us. Far ahead, I could see a few splotches which *might* be the airport at Daggett, our last stop before Los Angeles. I strained my eyes. How far? Seventy-five miles? In this air one cannot tell. My God that's the same peak there below us! Is there a head wind, a gale? Will we ever reach Daggett? The rocks are in my mouth and my heart beats hard. Don't fret, stupid, I *know* we have plenty of gas. A sort of desert hypnosis holds me, and I start to tremble. For five whole minutes, I promised myself, for five whole minutes, I will *not* look below. Now . . . count . . . wait; wait and wait . . . and when I look again I see that we have moved (a little) so Daggett must be (a little) nearer! How did any pioneer—ever—cross this awful land and reach the other side?

The sandy airstrip at Daggett-Gentry was a furnace, and at once we began to suffer. We had been so cool above the desert, and when I reached into the baggage compartment I was surprised that my suitcase felt chilled and icy. We took off up the hill, along a power line, down, along a railroad past some big Air Force bases, within sight of Apple Valley airport, and through the pass. There was Los Angeles, green and hazy. The desert was gone, and plants grew in the fields at the foot of the mountains. Then there were no more fields. Fly eight minutes due west, and then turn, and two minutes south, to Santa Monica. The dark, even expanse of ocean was ahead. The Santa Monica tower cleared us to land.

"Cortes," muttered Frederick as he closed the throttle. "Cortes, and us!"

That night I thought about all the things we had seen

and done, and specially about maps. I was always attracted by them, even as a child. They led my thoughts always farther on; there was nowhere I could not go, on a summer afternoon, flat on my stomach with an atlas in the shadow of the bushes. Now, many years later, it is the wing of an airplane under which I lie, and I still spread out my charts with a sigh of deep pleasure. I remember how I studied the colors of the maps, and how, for a time at least, I believed that the highest mountains had scarlet peaks, like hats; and, of course, the valleys were green and the rivers blue. I remembered this as we crossed the enormous rock pile east of Albuquerque, and I would not have been much surprised if the tops had been bright red! The little town of Needles, the Mohave Desert and the Colorado River, that looked so luscious and fertile in their rich green of the chart, were in real life so bare and grey and colorless. The river itself, which by all ordinary standards should be blue, was not even water! But if the colors on the charts were misleading and disappointing, there was much that we discovered in compensation. The plains of Oklahoma were, quite unexpectedly, a delicate patchwork of infinitely variable, nacreous hues. Utterly devoid of shape, the flatness seemed to emphasize the fine changes in the colors of the fields, conferring on the scene a special, subtle beauty. Farther west, the landscape became fantastic in shape and color. Once buried deep in the earth, visible now in the huge erosion gullies of the canyons, crude reds mix with purple, orange and green, accentuated by the shadows of the mountains.

"If we took any notice of this stuff," said the attendant as he stood high on the stepladder to reach the Stinson's wing tanks, "no one here would ever fly. We just go. We take off and climb out of it." Here was Los Angeles. Here was the ill-famed smog, caught in the basin of land where the city lies surrounded by a crescent of mountains, with the Pacific to the west. This was the first time I had seen smog. Early that morning I had waked to the certainty that something was important for the day . . . oh, yes, we planned to start the long trip home. I had peeked out of the window and seen the street lights like moons in the thick gloom, and at breakfast I read in the newspaper that the burning of trash was forbidden. How much, I wondered, would that help? Now, at midday, there were lighter places, suggestive of the sunshine above, and even that it might eventually break through. Perhaps we could find our way up and out of it. The tops were at fifteen hundred, the weatherman told us, and it was clear, everywhere but here; we planned to fly to Blythe and Phoenix and perhaps as far as Tucson. Visibilities were seventy-five miles, they said, and here less than three miles, which is the Civil Aeronautics minimum for contact flight.

We sat on the sofa in the airport office while we studied the course, plotted our check-points on the charts— and hesitated. In truth, I had plotted them many times before, and I had tried to imagine what they would look like in real life. I could do no more, sitting there waiting, while busy people came and went, the pilots of planes in the hangar, single-engined or twins. These people, I felt, had so much more experience than we. They probably all had instrument ratings and flew in any weather. So we mustn't appear as if we were looking for a "sucker hole" in the cloud cover. I study the chart as if it were new to me. We measure angles and distances and calculate gas consumption, trying to look important, as if we were in full control of the situation and ready to take off at any moment, whenever it suited us. But we knew it might be like this, for days.

At last, tired of inactivity, we went out to where the Stinson was waiting, sitting there all checked and full of fuel, baggage stowed away, a gallon of water in a plastic bag (I knew now that I was not foolish), even the abalone shell, unrestrained and almost vulgar in the exuberance of its colors, that I insisted on taking with us. That shell troubled Frederick, who could not understand why I wanted it; nor indeed could I, but I just knew that I did, and so I had wrapped it in some old rags and tucked it behind the baggage in the fuselage. As we stood there, the cloud layer thinned above us and we saw a shadow under a wing, there and gone again as we watched. It was enough, and by mutual unspoken consent we moved toward the airplane and opened the doors and climbed in, one on each side. We sat there, quiet for a moment, thinking of home. If, I thought —and this was a big if—the tower would clear us for take-off. Frederick started the engine and as we taxied up the long ramp I rechecked to be sure that I had the right charts, and that the one I needed first was folded and ready for use. We taxied on and on, and ahead of us were a Cessna and a twin Beechcraft waiting, and we could see the runway with planes landing, one after the other, hardly visible until they were suddenly down. The clouds darkened and I felt my heart beating hard. Once up in that mess, I thought, could we ever get down? What can we do, if we don't like it? I gripped the door handle. But it's all right a few miles away, I told myself, of course we'll go if they'll let us. The tower was very busy, chattering to the landing planes, and then the Cessna turned into position and took off. More delays, and then the Beechcraft was gone, into the stuff. There we waited, engine idling, close under the tower, watching the little figures high in the control room, listening for them, wondering when they were going to talk to us. There was a plane waiting behind us now.

"Stinson three two Kilo." He spoke slowly and with emphasis. "What are your intentions?" Honorable, or at least almost, I thought. Just give us clearance and let us go, please, and we'll be out of your way, out of this dense traffic, away over the desert. Visibility must be nearly three miles now, and we don't fly instruments, but you can't wait for it around here; nobody does. "Three two Kilo, cleared into position and hold." We moved and turned, facing down the runway, as an amphibian came in with a roar and landed low on its belly. "Three two Kilo," came the voice. "Your Flight Plan to Phoenix via Blythe is opened. Report when you leave the control zone. You are cleared for take-off. Over." This was it. The throttle went forward and the tail came up as we rushed down the runway and rose into the thick air. I looked at my watch, more from habit than anything else, and jotted down the time in my notebook. The Pacific Ocean was somewhere ahead of us,

I knew, but I could not see it, and as we turned back over the airport it looked very far away through the dirty haze. The Stinson, nose high, was circling, choosing the lightest places, and as we circled again, the airport and the houses around it were barely visible, and dirtier than ever. I hated to leave, but I hated not to! Oh! to get out above this mess! Up and still up, fifteen hundred, two thousand feet (hadn't that weather fellow said fifteen hundred?), and the stuff began to take form. Shoulders of thin cloud pushed close around us, and I saw clear spaces between and above them. Up and up we worked our way, round a cloud corner, over a cloud bridge, we were reaching, pulling upward, struggling to free ourselves. Then over another one, and round one more . . . and suddenly the world opened, crystal and cold. I caught my breath as high above us, in the bright blue sky, I saw a few sharp, white cirrus clouds, and far away were the mountains, gleaming as they poked out of a surface that was an endless expanse of grey mist, thickening over the sea.

What was it that had happened, in those last few feet of climbing, that changed the world, and me? For I became, most unreasonably, a different person. Somewhere inside me a gear shifted, and I was changed. Gone now is the tension, the fingers tight around the strut, the thumping heart, the eyes straining to see ahead, or to find a landmark below, a landing place in all that gloom. I sit aloft in security. How could an engine quit now, in that smooth, clear, firm air? Of course it could, but something in me tells me that it won't. It would be a betrayal, an indecency, a violation of the infinite beauty. I am bewitched and I know it, and yet I will go on that way forever. This is all I need of loveliness, loneliness; a little red airplane in a vast and shiny world. I will fly, forever.

"Come to your senses," said a voice in my ear, "and navigate! Which way do we go?" Oh, yes, charts, and the two great peaks that together make our first check-point, remember? We fly the pass between them. Those must be the ones. I check the compass heading, and switch the omnigator and move the tuner to pick up the frequency of the station to the south of us. I wiggle the dial, identify the station by its three call letters in Morse, and move the course selector until the needle centers and indicates our radial. The smog is clearing below us now and I can see the road and railroad running east, and that, with the radial, gives me the fix I need, and I know where I am. The two great peaks are nearer, towering into the blue sky, rising from sea level to almost eleven thousand feet within forty miles. They are the huge rock brothers, San Jacinto and San Gorgonio, with a pass between them that is said to develop turbulence more violent than any in the Rockies. So far, we were riding quietly, and the valley looked wide, wide enough for a turn if necessary, and there were several airports near us. So we planned to follow the pass, along the San Jacinto side, and see what would happen. We climbed some more and leveled off at eight thousand feet, still far below the two crests. Still no bumps. I tuned the dial to the omnirange at Thermal, our next check-point, but all I got was silence. The rocks of San Jacinto blocked the air between us and it, but as we came through the pass and round the corner over Palm Springs it burst upon us very loud, reporting the weather to anyone who would listen. Below us, instead of a land with many houses and few open spaces, the situation was reversed, and amid great stretches of yellow sand I could see tiny groups of houses. One of them, a little larger than the others, was Thermal, and there were mountain ranges on either side of the wide valley in which, far to the south, we could see the silver blue of a huge lake, the Salton Sea. The huge man-made expanse is below sea level, and in this region the altitude of the airports, always indicated on the chart just below the name, is preceded by a minus sign. "Thermal –117 L H 50." One hundred and seventeen feet down into the earth, I decoded; lights on the hard-surfaced runways, and the longest one was at least five thousand feet. We could see it, nearly two miles under us, but we still had plenty of gas in the tanks, so we turned east to follow the road to Blythe. I thought, how comfortable and cool I am, and how hot it must be down there. And this road-following is easy navigation, and a perfect opportunity for a sandwich. I unwrapped a package, and as we ate I noted a deserted airstrip on the roadside and checked its position on the chart. Then I tuned to the omnirange at Blythe, for our course led us directly over the station and I enjoy watching the antics of the needle. I knew what it would do. It would point steadily and determinedly toward the station until we got very close, and then it would lose control of itself and flounder back and forth as we passed over the tiny white omnirange hut, only to regain stability and settle down again soon after we were past. Now I could see the Colorado River, and the irrigated fields, a green smear in the distance. The big airport, on the western edge of the town, was in the desert; no half measures here: either there is water, or there is not. The fields were beautiful, oblong and of many shades of green. Across the river there are mountains, and over them is our way to Phoenix, but the road goes far to the north, and the chart shows almost nothing to navigate by. The desert heat came in on us as we lost altitude, and I noticed that the omni needle, which should have steadied after passing the station, was still wavering. That was odd, for it had worked all right since it had been repaired at Los Angeles. Had it really gone bad again so soon? Believe your omni and follow the needle, the experts told us, but I could not quite avoid an inner conviction that the old compass-check-point system was safer. It was here, over the lonely desert, that I had really planned to use the omni, wretched thing. I switched to Blythe control tower and we got clearance to land, and we gassed and took off at once. It was hot down there, a hundred and seven degrees, and I was glad to get up into the air again. People in cars, how they must feel! As we moved east over the river and the luscious green fields, the omni needle was still vacillating. We climbed straight out toward the mountain range, up and up, and the side of the mountain got nearer and nearer, and we were still far below the summit. "We are not going to make it," we said to each other, and Frederick turned north along the range. I looked up at the peaks. In spite of the Stinson's nose-high attitude and open throttle, we were not climbing; in fact we were going down! The needle of the sensitive altimeter unwound as I watched it, and we turned away from the mountainside, back and out over the river and fields. The nose was still up, and up! said the altimeter. Still nose high, we turned toward the range again, and, nose high, down we went! The wind, pouring like a waterfall from the high ridge into the valley, carried us down with it. We had heard of down drafts, and this was one of them. Gradually, making many spiral turns, little by little we gained on it and rose, until it no longer pushed at us, and we turned once more, and set off on our compass course for Phoenix.

Only an hour and a half, and Phoenix is a large town with an abundance of landing fields. I counted at least thirty on the chart, from tiny emergency strips in the desert to the huge Skyharbor and Luke Air Force Base, where jets congregate. And Phoenix is on the Gila River, fat and blue on the chart, so whatever we do we will come eventually to the river; we can't miss, I thought. And we'll pick up the omni at Hassayampa, too; the machine ought to work. We really couldn't get lost. But the road was soon out of sight, winding its way through a pass far to the north . . . it must be a long way round by road. We were over mountains and they were everywhere, sharp, high peaks alternating with flat tops, and already the Blythe omni had faded out. On the charts of this land they mark even the wells and the water holes. I thought with satisfaction of our gallon water bag. Those desolate crags, four in a row across our path, those must be the Eagle Tail Mountains, so we *are* a bit north of our course. If we don't pick up the omnirange, we'll keep a little south—just then I hear it. "Hassayampa-unattended-omni-Hassayampa-unattended-omni-Hassayampa-unattended-omni" it repeats in an endless monotone, far out in the wilderness. Our needle heard Hassayampa, too. That way, it said, and steadied itself, and pointed to the north of our eastward heading. No that's not the way to go, I told it, you are wrong, at the Eagle Tails we were north, so over there, that's it. No landmarks, nothing, but somehow I feel sure. What a way to navigate, to believe the needle only when it says what you want it to say! But what of the gyrations at Blythe? It may well be crazy, and I'd be better with the old familiar compass, and my own instinct. And if we are south of our course, as the omni tells me, why don't we find the river? It's time we reached it, by my watch, and we haven't, so we must be north just as I thought, in spite of the wretched needle. "You are south of Hassayampa unattended omni, you are past it but south, too far south . . ." it repeated in its own sign language. "Remember Blythe!" I told it. The minutes are very long when you don't know quite where you are, and infinitely long over desert. Then, away to the northeast of us, far away I saw a faint haze, with the shapes of objects in it, man-made shapes. Whatever it was, we could go and see, for in this land anything man-made would have an airport nearby. It couldn't be a mirage, could it? Then I saw a small, thin road which crossed some rough places on a sort of viaduct. I could see the arches supporting the roadbed. Arches? Why arches? To let water through . . . but there wasn't any water . . . unless . . . it was the river bed down there, waterless now and dry. I had been fooled, and the needle had been right after all! We turned and followed the rocky, winding path, and soon we reached Phoenix and landed.

A half hour later we were off again, and the air cooled as we headed south for Tucson. Navigating was simple here, for there were roads and cultivated land and groups of houses in the valley. The colors deepened in the low evening sunlight, green and purple in layers, and red and orange on the mountainsides. We slid onward, turned around a bluff into a narrow funnel between the ranges, and through a pass. By now, the mountains ahead were purple, darkening to inky black as we flew over the town for the last landing of the day. At the motel, palm trees and tall cactus grew around the pool where we swam. We ate, and then lay on the sand, utterly relaxed, in starlight that seemed brighter and sweeter than any I had ever known.

Next day, en route to El Paso, we passed over salt flats, where the lonely operator of Salt Flats Radio wished us a pleasant trip. There were small, dead volcanos, and some very high ridges. "Caution," reads the notice on the chart. "The reliability of relief information, covering the Mexican area, is questionable, and all elevations should be used with caution." Grey-greenness was everywhere now, dense growth like thick moss, a mile below us, and with no paths for men or cattle. A thin, straight line was the great border fence, and the Stinson followed the fence, one wing in Mexico, for many miles. To the north, far away, a line of towering cumulus clouds lay on the horizon, parallel with our course. To the south was Mexico, but I saw only mountains and sand, and greenish scrub, and once a strange mushroom-shaped object, very far away. Dust? A geyser? Presently we listened, as usual, to the aviation weather broadcast, and heard a report of thunder and heavy rain squalls at Amarillo, only a hundred miles from us, under those towering cumulus, I supposed. That line was a front, we decided. We would go as far as we could, and get well ahead of it.

More hills and endless bare miles, before the landscape changed a little. The mountains were gone, and here and there were big smoke plumes and oil derricks. The towns, covered with small dark green trees, contrasted with the brown land. Midland, Abilene; the country grew populated again. We made a record flight that day, and landed at Dallas in a fierce gale, just before dark. But the front caught up with us in the night, and went over us, and to the east. We followed it for a week, jumping this way and that, stopping when it stopped and moving when it moved. It stuck, as fronts often do, on the Alleghenies, and we waited behind it. But, at last, the stuff cleared from the mountaintops, and we flew home.

Of the many impressions on our six-thousand-mile journey, I count as greatest the ease and comfort of our progress over distances which seemed long only on the charts. There would be, perhaps, three hundred miles between one airport and the next; two and a half hours aloft, spent either navigating, with never quite enough time to absorb the ever-changing scenes, or gazing around, without quite as much time as I would like for navigating. The air was always clean and cool. Always, too, there was on every flight, a sort of fresh sensation, an alertness in the blood, both in doubtful weather, when I like to know every minute exactly where I am, or under clear, open skies, when the check-points appear on schedule and getting lost is no problem.

All the way, the good Franklin engine sang steadily in our ears. It sings a welcome song, one that becomes a natural part of the day, and only intrudes upon you when (if) it isn't there! Our engine never missed a beat. When the clouds were low, it purred with extra sweetness in the moisture-laden air. "I'll do my part," I have heard it whisper, "and you do yours. Don't bother about me, I'm all right."

All the way, I was never for a moment bored. Occasionally, I was disturbed and tense, but only for a short time, and I found that even those times were worth while, in terms of experience gained. I would not have had it otherwise.

I hope, someday soon, we'll fly west again.

CHAPTER 10

S *aturday* afternoon is the nicest time at the Airport-on-
the-Hill. Ever since I started to fly, Saturday has been
airport day. At first I would ride eagerly as Frederick's
passenger; then came lessons, and all the delightful things
that have happened since. Now that I instruct, Saturday
has become the most important teaching day. Sometimes,
of course, Frederick and I go off in the Stinson for the
weekend, but more often Sunday is the day for trips to
the coast or to the mountains, and Saturday is left for

another sort of flying, a sort that I enjoy as much as any. I potter about the airport. I do chores for the airplanes, washing or waxing them, changing oil. There may be hangar-flying in progress, or local flying gossip to discuss; or we just sit and watch the take-offs and landings. Usually I take a student for an hour of instruction, and we may visit a nearby airport, talk awhile, and fly back as dusk falls. Or I plan some small repair job . . . and usually three or four young men gather to watch me, and soon they offer (even insist) that they do it for me. Then, if they are not airplane owners, I offer them a ride. The airport is a wonderfully friendly place, and I go there, not for excitement (nowadays planes are too reliable for that) but for the pure pleasure of being with airplanes and the people who love them. And I don't really care how much or how little I fly. Just once round the pattern is all it takes to allay the thwarted, fretful imprisonment of a grounded Saturday.

When I arrive, and drive my car up the hill into the parking area, I look around, anticipating. I look at the hangar and its wind sock. I glance at the cars, and note strange aircraft which may be parked on the grass, or any signs of unusual activity. No one can ever predict what will happen at the Hill. Take, for instance, the Saturday of the prairie lark. For several weeks I had noticed that a bird ran away into the tall grass as I walked down the steps to the hangar. Presently I found its nest, a cup-shaped structure on the open ground, under a weed. Then the five eggs hatched, and every time I started the Aeronca, I carefully turned the tail away, so that the little birds would not be blown out of their home by the blast of the propeller. Once I sat down on the ground by the nest, determined to protect it from a Piper Cruiser which taxied round the hangar. I don't know what the pilot thought! The chicks grew. They sat quite still, unaware of their precarious location, their tiny comical faces peering over the edge of the nest, their beaks forming a five-pointed star. Each bird had tufted whiskers (unbelievably big for anything so small) which touched the whiskers of the next, stiff and bristly, giving them an appearance of perpetual surprise. I told no one of my secret.

The next time I arrived, I looked down from the bank onto a whole crowd of people! Oh, I thought, they've trampled my birds! But they were a group of learned ornithologists, who had come to see the nest of the prairie lark, the first ever found in North Carolina! The next day, two young birds had left, and soon the nest was empty. I hoped they would come back next year to use the fine man-made prairie, but if they did I never saw them.

On Saturdays in the fall, in the football season, the airport is crowded with visitors who have flown, often for long distances, to attend the game. I have seen as many as a hundred planes, from shiny twin-engined beauties to battered Cubs, lined up in neat rows on the grass. They arrive at intervals during the morning, but after the game they leave with a rush. First, often before the game is over, the press photographers come running out with their cameras, and jump into their planes, and are gone. Then come the others, and as the propellers whirr, they taxi out in a long procession, waddling along close behind one another, and they take off like bubbles rising into the evening sky. Many of them tuck up their wheels as they clear the ground, and, graceful as birds, hurry away into the sunset. We are left, to close up the hangar and go home. Sometimes one or two planes will still be there, and we chock the wheels before we leave, in case of wind. I think these belong to wise pilots who, having enjoyed the game too well, wait until morning to take off.

Even when there is no football, visiting planes come and buy gas, and the pilots talk awhile. Mostly, they are a pleasant group. One day, though, an Ercoupe flew in to visit us, bringing two young men, strangers. It was a hot Saturday, and several of us were sitting in the shade, relaxed and lazy, a group of pilots who knew and respected one another, ready to help one another if needed, or mind our own business. I sat on the turf in the shade of the Aeronca wing, and looked at maps with my two students. We talked of cross-country work, for one of them was soon to go off by himself; the other was a girl who had never flown before, and I planned to take her up later. Several other planes were on the concrete apron, their owners taking turns with the hose, spraying the surfaces so that the clear beads of water glittered in the sun before they dried. "Hot Pilot" Howard was polishing something, and his wife and little boy were helping. Eric the Navigator was there, and had, as usual, a pretty girl at his side. We felt friendly together in the pleasant warmth, and strange pilots were welcome to join us.

I did not see the Ercoupe before it landed, but I

saw it taxi, very fast, onto the apron. It came straight toward the parked planes, and swerved sharply away, just in time to avoid a collision. Then, with a burst of throttle, it blew dust and scraps all over the newly washed planes, and two young men came out of it, loudly demanding gasoline. While the tank was being filled they strode, bold and uninvited, into the hangar, where they pulled on a propeller, kicked at a tire, opened a plane door and slammed it shut. We watched, unfriendly, even hostile now. "If we don't feed them," muttered someone near me, "maybe they'll go away." Presently they were ready to leave. "Contact!" yelled the pilot, and his companion went to work, whirling legs and arms. Nothing happened, and we watched, until presently his forehead dripped with sweat, but still nothing happened. They changed places and the pilot worked and no one offered to help him. They changed places again. At last I was anxious to see them go. "Look," I said, "I have some Ercoupe time. If you like, I will try to start it." The pilot climbed out with a shrug. With my head deep in the cockpit, I fiddled with the controls, and set them in a position which sometimes will catch an engine which is hot and flooded with gas. I held the brakes. "Contact!" and it started.

Now it is hard, I know, for a young and newly licensed aviator to accept help from a woman, so I was not surprised or unduly vexed when they left without a word. I thought no more of them until, after the takeoff with my new student, I saw the Ercoupe coming toward me. I turned back around the field, and it came up, behind, and I was sure now that it was chasing me. It came very close, behind and a little below, and there was nothing I could do. It got so close that I could see the faces in the cockpit as they laughed together and grinned up at me. I raged, but I was helpless. My plane was slower than theirs, and I had to watch for other traffic, and fly, too. I thought of making a quick swerve to scare them, but it was too dangerous. Oh, for a pot of boiling oil, or a long whip! All I could do was to fly straight ahead and pray that the pilot would not come closer. But I could get down and report them; this was a forbidden maneuver, and they knew it. I'd get the CAA after them, and how! I raged and fumed as I lost altitude, and they were still there, right on my tail. I made my final turn and landed, going far down the runway, with the Ercoupe following me. But then it stopped following, and turned, with its usual excessive speed, back again for another take-off, as if in a hurry to get away. Then, out of control, it went around in a ground loop, and there was a crash and a tearing sound, as a wing tip broke against a pine tree on the bank. They taxied to the hangar, now two forlorn young men, grounded, with a borrowed Ercoupe. So much deflated, they seemed, that my indignation faded away. They had learned more, that afternoon, than the CAA could teach them. The Ercoupe stayed at the field for several weeks until its owner arrived with a new wing, and flew it away.

It was after the California trip that I started instructing regularly, and it was then that I began to learn how to teach. As with any skill which has become automatic, the correction and explanation of mistakes is at first quite difficult. Students would meet me at the airport, one or two on a Saturday afternoon, as I used to meet George, long ago.

We talk as we check the plane, in a careful pre-flight routine. There is a challenge in being careful, for omissions are serious. Check the gasoline and oil, and see that the tank caps are in place. Drain the carbureter water trap. Note the conditions of the tires and tail-wheel assembly. Controls in working order? Cowling tight? Gas turned on? All this I emphasize.

One day Willie the Aeronca was at the fuel pit, and a student and the attendant filled the tank while two young men stood idly watching. I went to fetch some oil. "Put that cap on the gas tank!" I called as I came back round the corner of the hangar, much too far away to see what they were doing. A stir came over the astonished group of young men, and admiring glances came my way! For weeks they teased me to know how I sensed what they had done, but I wouldn't tell them, for I didn't know!

For the first few lessons I handle the controls for take-offs and landings, and for all flight near the ground. At two thousand feet or more, where there is altitude for recovery if the plane goes out of control, I tell the student to take the stick and rudders, and find out for himself what they will do. Straight and level flight, and glides, climbs and turns, are his first concern. On these flights the beginner struggles with the controls; he holds on tightly. His muscles are tense and so he pulls back and sideways on the stick, and we climb, often with the right wing low. "Watch your wings! Level them with the horizon! . . . No, put the nose down, you're still climbing! That's better; now we are level. *Now* climb! More throttle, set your nose on that cloud and hold right rudder against the propeller torque! Keep it straight!" . . . and so on. Climb, level, glide, level, changing from one to the other. With a good student, I push him. Do this, don't forget that! Be quick! But I have not forgotten the old days and how I struggled, and how tired I used to get. So from my back seat I try to recognize the signs, little ones sometimes, of strain; a hand brushing across a forehead, or an exasperated shake of the head, or just some unco-ordinated turns, worse instead of better than the last ones. Then I take over. "You relax," I say. "I'll fly it and show you something." I like to see him wriggle and settle down. His neck and shoulders, where they join, seem to come suddenly lose from each other. Now is the time, I think, to close the throttle and make him do a simulated forced landing, but he's been working very hard. We'll do that next time. So instead I ease back on the throttle and stick, and pull the plane up until it is almost stalled. It will fly like this, perfectly well, at forty-five miles an hour, nose high, with the controls getting wobbly; mushing, we call it, or Slow Flight. No one in his right mind would ordinarily fly that way, but it is good practice for a student. And then it is easy, with slightly greater back pressure on the stick, to bring about a stall. I always enjoy Slow

Flight; facing a high wind you can sit in the air over a farmhouse and five minutes later the house is still under you, and sometimes the plane will even move backwards over the ground.

Gradually, the struggling beginner finds out for himself that which I cannot tell him, the amount of pressure which is required on the stick and rudders to produce a turn or climb. Then he finds that he is flying the plane, better than it can fly without him. "You are in charge," I tell him. "Be accurate! Make it fly where *you* want it to go!" And about this time, my position behind him gets more comfortable, as his co-ordination improves. In an airplane, the center of gravity is not far behind the engine, and in the back seat the effect of a poorly executed turn is very marked. Even small slips or skids are perceptible to the instructor, who relies on that traditional built-in bank-and-turn indicator, the seat of his (her) pants!

Then there are stalls. Stalls shall be practiced, says the Civil Aeronautics Administration, "out of all anticipated flight attitudes." Stalls with power on; the sort of stall which might occur in a too-steep pull-up after take-off; power-off stalls, the sort you do every time you land. Stalls out of climbing turns or out of gliding ones, and these, specially, I enjoy. Engine throttled back, we glide, quietly in a gentle turn. Pull back on the stick, I tell the student, back, more back, while it turns. One wing is lifted high and the other dips. Pull back some more, nose up! Suddenly, the airflow breaks from the low wing; it stalls, and a shudder spreads over the whole airplane.

It staggers and starts to fall. Stick forward, and throttle forward, and the pilot is in control again.

Sometimes, as I sit behind a student, secure and with dual controls if I have to correct his errors, I wonder about the old days, and how it must have been then. All by himself, in a large field or sandy flat, the would-be pilot taxied back and forth, faster and faster, learning the feel of the airplane. Then he became bold. Facing the wind, he opened the throttle, and slammed it shut again as soon as he had left the ground. Straight ahead at first, and then maybe a gentle turn. A very gentle turn, for in those days, if you stalled, you went into a spin. And that was the end, for no one had ever recovered from one.

There are two aspects of the flying game, the dangers of which I impress upon my students. They are those of a whirring propeller and of collision in the air. The power behind a turning propeller is terrific, and it is invisible, for the tips move almost as fast as sound, too fast for the eye to see. People have been known to walk right into them. Pilots, starting an engine by turning the propeller, must know just what to watch for, because airplanes are unpredictable and will play the meanest tricks. I have seen and heard of many avoidable accidents, and near accidents, too. The Cessna 140, whose owner pulled the prop without chocking it, escaped and went berserk on the ramp and chewed up its twin. They fought like dogs, going round and round before they could be stopped. And I knew of an Ercoupe that committed suicide in the bushes. A friend with many flying hours came with me to fly the Stinson. The battery was weak, so I got out to pull it through. "Off?" I cried, and "Off!" came the reply. Even so, I thought, I'll treat it as if it were hot. I pulled it and it started, and although I was ready for it, I jumped back, tripped and fell, safely but ungracefully, into a pile of grass and rocks! My companion spent a few bad moments before we got sorted out. The master switch *was* off. But he did not know that it had nothing to do with the magneto switch, which was on!

Up in the sky there is plenty of space. It is lonely. A cross-country trip of many hours can be accomplished, in good visibility, without ever seeing another aircraft. And yet things happen. A plane coming toward you leaves little time for action. In the distance, hidden against the mottled trees and fields, they are often very difficult to see, and to keep in sight. You find one, and a moment later it is lost, then found again. Sometimes you can trace it by its shadow. Perhaps you will see one, moving over the boundary of the airport, and then a plane follows it; they get closer and closer together, to meet and unite at touchdown.

Alone in the Stinson, I was on my way to an airport about an hour distant. I was flying low, at less than two thousand feet, out over flatlands and lonely meadows. The airplane flew itself, and I sat there relaxed, but as usual I turned my head from side to side to watch for other traffic. I took a large hard candy ball from my handbag, undid the wrapper and put the ball into my mouth. I sucked the sharp, synthetic flavor and allowed it to creep up the back of my nose, and as I did so, I took an extra good look all around me, even behind as far as I could see. Then I laughed to myself; I was actually slightly uneasy that someone might see me. Since the very early days when they were contraband, jawbreakers are to be relished in strict privacy. In those days, they were bought with pennies at the village store, and smuggled home and into the attic. But no one had seen me, and I sucked noisily.

There, crossing the big meadow below me, was the shadow of an airplane! I sat up, tense. The shadow moved fast; it was huge; for an instant, I thought it was mine, but it was to the south and beside me, and so was the sun. It couldn't be mine! I knew it couldn't! Panic seized me, and I could hardly breathe. It was a shadow, so it was cast by something. There must be an airplane, very close, much too close to me, and I couldn't find it. I noticed that the shadow had several points on it, and a long one, the nose? A multi-engined plane. Close above me, or below? I peered on all sides and up and down, afraid to lift a wing or turn from my straight course. Some gigantic creature was in the sky above me . . . and then I saw it, a four-motored jet with swept-back wings, and it darted close below, grey and drab in color, and fierce. Low down over the trees it sped away, and its shadow followed it, leaping up and down.

It happened on a Saturday, but I did not begin to suspect the truth until more than a week later. The weather was wonderfully fine and quiet, and I was at the airport every afternoon, flying, or sitting in the sun chatting with students and with the two instructors, Poppa and old Walter Whitcombe. I liked to hear Walt tell of his early flying days soon after the first world war, especially of his affair with a lovely, willful and treacherous Curtiss-Jenny. I listened gladly and respectfully to the two "grand old men." Why is there no phrase, yet, to describe such people? Sailors invented one long ago, but since man learned to fly there has not been much time, and the words I wanted are still missing. Poppa and Walt, both genuine old-timers—airmen through and through. With his blue eyes and his firmly set jaw, Poppa stood upright, stocky and straight, a match for anything. Walt, at first impression, seemed almost indolent, he was so tall and stooped. I used to wonder how his long, rangy legs found space in the cockpit of his tiny Cessna. Then, suddenly, his lazy movements were gone, and his eyes would gleam with fire and his whole body would shorten at the thought of flying. He was a meticulous pilot, I knew; a perfectionist, and I was sorry indeed for the student of his who made a stupid mistake.

The morning of the Saturday it happened, I had flown Walt in the Stinson to Westington to get his Cessna, which had been there a week for repairs. Ferrying, we call it. The pilots around the airport often do this for one another, for it saves us long and dreary journeys by car. His plane was ready. As we stood there an old friend of Walt's came out of the office, an instructor who had known him at a big wartime teaching base, long before I learned to fly. Talking and reminiscing, they presently went to lunch together, while I took off for home.

"Tell them I'll be back in an hour or two," Walt called.

Tuesday, it must have been, that someone brought me a cutting from a local paper, and I read it with mild interest. "A single-engined plane ran out of gas, and the pilot landed it in a field of onions just south of Elton. The onions were spoiled but the plane was not damaged. The pilot, an elderly man, refused to identify himself."

That afternoon at the airport, the story was repeated. No one I know, I told the students. I wondered who it might be. Maybe Walt or Poppa would know. But they were both flying, so we speculated. How could such a thing happen, we asked, something so easily avoided with ordinary care? It sounded like an expert landing, though the reports of newspapers are often not accurate. At the office, I mentioned it to the caretaker. No, he hadn't heard of it. Presently Walt landed the Cessna in front of us, and as he touched down with three-point elegance, his wheels hit against the hard flowering heads of the wild onions which grow among the grasses on the runways. I could hear them bumping as he taxied. He sat beside us.

"Place needs mowing," said someone. "Those onions are ready to harvest. How they smell!"

Like a cat, every muscle alerted by a movement in the undergrowth, Walt's eyes hardened and his neck stiffened as he turned to watch the faces in the group, seeking for a reason, where there was none. Ignorance and innocence were all he found, and the discharge from his inner battery quickly faded. I was aware of this, without understanding.

Onions? It was all so improbable, so very unlikely, that the situation had yet to force itself upon me.

Then on Thursday, at the big airport, I heard it again. What was this, they asked? An instructor from the Hill had a forced landing, out of gas? Still I shook my head. Silly rumors flourish among pilots!

Now there lives a man in the village, who is also a pilot of the old days. He doesn't fly now, but I often drop in for a chat, for the sake of the little bits of airplane lore I can pick up. He shows me photographs of the biplanes he used to fly, and we talk of performance, maneuvers and short field landings.

"Have you seen Walt lately?" I asked him. "Not since Saturday," he said. "Queer thing. He and his wife were to come to play bridge at six, and it was a quarter of nine before they came. They made no explanation. Seemed rather disturbed."

Silently, I reached into my handbag and pulled out the scrap of newspaper. I handed it to him. As he read, I watched his face. Finally, he looked up, and I knew that each of us knew!

"You don't suppose, do you?"

"And he didn't say a word! Not a word!"

"Poor Walt," I said. "That's really hard!" And we both smiled. *Don't you be so smug,* I said to myself. *It might have been you!*

The next time we met, Walt was ready and fully composed, but his lips were tight.

"Do you know, I forgot to fill it up on Saturday after

you left," he said casually. "Over Elton the engine cut, and I knew right away. Just got it in over the fence. No trouble landing. We had to take the wings off before we could get it out. And I had to pay for the onions. What a mess! Guess I was lucky, at that!"

Toward the end of a flight, on a quiet evening, I get out from my seat behind a student and tell him to solo. Then, with sinking heart, I watch my little Willie rush across the field and away and up, without me. . . . Oh! how easily it climbs, so lightly loaded now. Helpless, I fret and turn away; I wonder why ever I let him go. I walk in circles on the grass, or wander restlessly through the hangar. The plane takes much too long to fly the pattern. I listen. Why don't I hear it? I look. There it is, high and tiny in the distance, and then I hear the engine, the sound growing louder as it approaches. With relief, I see the plane over the trees, almost down. But he's bringing it in *much* too fast! Just as I am sure that he has forgotten all I ever told him, and will crash horribly into the ground, he levels off and is down. My spirits rise as I wave him on, to go round again.

Each time I solo a student, I suffer, and a small part of me is torn away and flies with him. Have I taught him to the best of my ability? What have I not emphasized? What would he do, if an emergency came his way? May I say of him (as airmen do in highest praise of one another), "He can look after himself"? And if I suffer, and if the responsibility of teaching is sometimes a heavy load, what then, I ask myself, do I want with an instructor's ticket, and the Aeronca, a trainer plane? It is a question to which I know the answer. I fly for fun, and I want others to have fun, too. If I can give anyone a chance to fly, that is what I want to do. I want to share Willie, and the joy I have in him, with others. So, when the plane goes off without me, and I stay on the ground and fret, I know that it is part of what I want, and what I enjoy; part of a delightful game.

At last, at long last, a student will complete the requirements for the Private license. The written exam is passed and the solo hours are recorded in his logbook; the maneuvers, the cross-country flights are all completed. I sign a recommendation, and he flies off in the Aeronca to take his flight test.

It was a Saturday in July that my first student, Jim, planned his flight test with the inspector at Westington. So with his wife and children and some other friends we gathered at the airport for a picnic supper, to greet him on his return. The evenings in summer are long and usually quiet, but this Saturday the wind blew hard. At midday, I had called the Weather Bureau. East-northeast, they told me; eighteen knots and gusts up to twenty-five, but they thought it would not increase. That is about as much wind as a light plane can manage; the gusts make taxiing difficult. We watched it, Jim and I, for a while before we pulled the Aeronca from the hangar. I thought: I have confidence in Jim. He is a good pilot, and can handle it. And so he flew away.

Toward evening we brought hampers and spread rugs on the grass, under a bank of pines near the hangar,

protected from the wind. We could see the runway and
the wind sock, with the sock still pushed out stiffly, the
tip wandering from side to side. Frederick, in the Stinson, flew three passengers over the town, and presently
he came back and reloaded, and went off again. The
heavy, solid Stinson, with four people, does not dance and
skitter in the wind. Jim should be back soon; he had been
gone a long time. We sorted packages, and arranged
the food, while the children begged for marshmallows and
hot dogs. The Stinson came, and left again, and still the
wind blew. And still we waited. At last a tiny speck
appeared in the western sky. I saw it, and lost it, and
found it again. How tiny it was! Slowly, very slowly,
it grew larger, until there was no doubt that it was an
airplane, fighting its way into the wind. Old slowpoke
Willie, battling the gale! Did it fly happily, I wondered?
Was the trip a success?

Slowly the airplane worked its way upstream, sometimes almost seeming to stand still, pushing hard against
the wind. At last it was directly over us, and it hesitated,
rocking its wings as a signal of triumph to us who stood
there below. Then it was caught and flung sideways, as
a leaf is tossed and whirled away in a rushing current.
Instantly, it was back, over the border of the field again,
turning, even as it was carried away, to face the wind
once more for the final struggle. I ran out to watch. I
was there, up there with Jim, helping him fly, sharing
his exaltation in the battle. The strategy was planned.
Speed, speed at any price, either dive or throttle, or both.
And wings level. What if the gale strikes . . . wham!

. . . and then lets go suddenly, and the bottom goes out between you and the oaks? Then your speed saves you from a stall. What if the attack is from the side? Quick, put the wing down and head back to the runway. I saw him lose altitude, then rise again. Nose low he came then, almost onto the runway, fast. The airplane dipped, floated, and as it tried to fly again, the wheels touched. Flying speed gone, it stopped suddenly, and then it taxied slowly forward into the protection of the lee side of the hangar. Jim cut the engine and climbed out, his face alight with the joy of the windy landing and the good news I knew already. Darkness and the stars came fast as we talked and he told us all about it. He had worked hard. In the strong and gusty wind he had done the best he could. The inspector had congratulated him. At last I heard the sound I was listening for, and always rejoice to hear, the distinctive high whine of the Franklin engine. Our Stinson, with its big tail high and black, its navigation lights shining on the wing tips, came over us and into the pattern, with the last glow of the sunset behind it. The tip lights spread wider and wider apart as it came in over the trees, its wings moving up and down like those of a huge bat. The struts whistled their special landing tune. The beam of the floodlight flashed on, and it was down. We pushed it into the hangar and shut the big doors. For a long time we sat and talked in the cool night, while a great owl hunted mice and the pines murmured around us. At last we carried the sleeping children to the cars, and went home.